THE
Little Women
TREASURY

THE
Little Women
TREASURY

Carolyn Strom Collins

Christina Wyss Eriksson

VIKING

VIKING
Published by the Penguin Group
Penguin Books USA Inc., 375 Hudson Street, New York, New York 10014, U.S.A.
Penguin Books Ltd, 27 Wrights Lane, London W8 5TZ, England
Penguin Books Australia Ltd, Ringwood, Victoria, Australia
Penguin Books Canada Ltd, 10 Alcorn Avenue, Toronto, Ontario, Canada M4V 3B2
Penguin Books (N.Z.) Ltd, 182–190 Wairau Road, Auckland 10, New Zealand

Penguin Books Ltd, Registered Offices: Harmondsworth, Middlesex, England

First published in 1996 by Viking Penguin, a division of Penguin Books USA Inc.

1 3 5 7 9 10 8 6 4 2

LIBRARY OF CONGRESS CATALOGING IN PUBLICATION DATA
Collins, Carolyn Strom.
The Little women treasury / by Carolyn Strom Collins and Christina Wyss Eriksson.
p.   cm.
ISBN 0-670-86337-8
1. Alcott, Louisa May, 1832–1888.   Little women.   2. New England—Social life and customs—
19th century.   3. New England—In literature.   I. Eriksson, Christina Wyss.   II. Title.
PS1017.L53C65   1996
813´.4—dc20   96-11034

This book is printed on acid-free paper.
∞

Printed in the United States of America
Set in Berkeley Book
Book design by Beth Tondreau
Art direction by Jaye Zimet

For our treasured daughters,
our own "little women"—
Caroline and Sarah Jane

ACKNOWLEDGMENTS

We very much appreciate the attention and expertise of the staff of the Louisa May Alcott Memorial Association, especially Heather C. Wager, assistant to the director for collections and preservations; Marcia Moss of the Concord Free Library Archives; Doug Sabin, historian, and Scott Collum of the Minute Man National Historical Park in Concord; the docents at the Ralph Waldo Emerson House; the staff at the Concord Museum; the staff at the Fruitlands Museum in Harvard, Massachusetts; and the librarians at Houghton Library, Harvard University. Their impressive knowledge about the Alcott family, their friends, and their times added significantly to our interpretation of the world of Louisa May Alcott's *Little Women*.

To our editors, Jane von Mehren and Tamar Mendelson, and our literary agent, Jeanne Hanson, we extend our thanks and admiration.

As always, to our husbands, Andy and Mark, and our children, Caroline and Drew, Aaron and Sarah Jane, we offer much gratitude and love—your interest in and enthusiasm about this project have made all the difference.

—C.S.C. and C.W.E.

CONTENTS

INTRODUCTION

Though the themes of Louisa May Alcott's *Little Women*—coming of age, developing self-knowledge, overcoming personal faults, female independence—are universal and speak as eloquently to readers of today as they did well over a hundred years ago, some of the details in the lives of Meg, Jo, Beth, and Amy might need a bit of explanation and elaboration for the modern reader. After all, how many of us still stitch monograms on linen handkerchiefs, cook biscuits and tarts in wood-burning ovens, iron yards and yards of long skirts and petticoats with flatirons, or put hot turnovers (or "muffs," as the March girls called them) in our pockets to keep our hands warm for a long, cold walk into town?

As we laugh and cry with the sisters over their everyday pranks and problems, sigh with them over their dreams of wealth, fame, homes of their own, or just "being good," we also cherish the possibility of living in their world, if only for a few moments.

In *The Little Women Treasury,* we have chosen some of the elements from Louisa May Alcott's *Little Women*, *Little Men*, and *Jo's Boys* that will show today's readers more about how the March girls lived and how to do many of the things they enjoyed, such as cooking their favorite dishes, planting some of the flowers they grew in their gardens, making some of the gifts they made for each other, and much more.

Since Louisa based her *Little Women* series largely on her own family's home life, we began our search for clues to the Marches' world at the Alcott home, Orchard House, in Concord, Massachusetts. The Alcotts lived there from 1858 to 1877; Louisa wrote *Little Women* there in 1868. We learned a great deal about the house and the Alcotts' life there and how much of it fit in with Louisa's stories. To set the scene for *The Little Women Treasury*, we drew a floor plan for Orchard House as it existed when Louisa wrote *Little Women*, based on F. C. Detwiller's research on the history of the house and its stages of construction and remodeling, along with notes from Bronson Alcott's journals and Louisa's descriptions of the house in the books. This floor plan, and its accompanying site plan showing the locations of some of the other landmarks from *Little Women* (some real, some imaginary), should help the reader visualize more clearly the setting for *Little Women*.

From Alcott family journals, letters, keepsakes, and pictures, we discovered that many of the things we loved about the world of *Little Women* actually existed in the Alcotts' lives, including the family post office, the Pickwick Club badges and newsletters, the ever-present gingerbread, monogrammed handkerchiefs and other needlework, even the famous sausage pillow on the parlor sofa. Studying these artifacts, so carefully and lovingly preserved first by Louisa's family and now by the museum, we found we could give today's readers very definite instructions for duplicating many of the March girls' favorite things.

Some of the other elements of the stories had to be re-created based on other sources: magazines and books from the late 1800s yielded much information on the flowers and gardens, recipes and handicrafts of the period. Visits to many museums, libraries, and archives, as well as interviews with experts on various topics, gave us more insights into how many things were done in the *Little Women* era.

In addition to describing the Marches' world, we also wanted to give readers an idea of what the rest of the world was like in the twenty-eight years the *Little Women* series took place, from just before the beginning of the Civil War to the year 1888, also the year of Louisa's death. Many important world events happened and inventions we still use today debuted in those years. Some of these, along with births and deaths of influential people from that era, are noted year by year in the context of the incidents that occurred in the series.

We hope that *The Little Women Treasury* will inspire many readers not only to create for themselves some portion of the world of Meg, Jo, Beth, and Amy, but also to learn more about Louisa May Alcott and her legacy.

Louisa May Alcott
and the
Little Women
Books

Louisa May Alcott

(1832–1888)

*L*ittle Women is not, of course, an autobiography, but much of the story is rooted in Louisa May Alcott's life. One of the most important reasons for the book's appeal is that it grew out of Louisa's deep feelings for the people and places she knew and the experiences she had. Louisa suggests as much herself, through the words of Mr. March, in Part Second of *Little Women*, written shortly after Part First had been received with such overwhelming success in 1868:

> "There is truth in it, Jo, that's the secret; humor and pathos make it alive, and you have found your style at last."

Louisa wrote *Little Women* when she was thirty-five years old. By that time, she had already lived a most unusual life as part of an impressive and nontraditional family.

Louisa was born on November 29, 1832, in Germantown, Penn-

Abigail and Bronson Alcott

sylvania, a little community outside of Philadelphia. Louisa's father, Bronson Alcott, was in charge of a school there. Her sister, Anna, who was a year older, was quiet and easy to manage, but Louisa was headstrong, adventurous, and full of energy. She was more like her mother, Abigail, who was descended from the prominent May family of Boston.

When Louisa was two years old, the Alcotts moved to Boston, where Bronson started his own school. Even at her young age, Louisa managed to explore the city, running and playing on the Boston Commons and watching the big ships being unloaded down the hill in the harbor. She also spent a great deal of time with her May cousins who lived nearby on Beacon Hill. Anna preferred to spend time at home with her mother and new baby sister, Elizabeth who was born in 1835.

After living in Boston for five years, the Alcotts moved to the small village of Concord about twenty miles west of the city. Bronson had given up teaching and had decided to develop his interest in philosophy. In Concord, he would be in the midst of a group of writers and intellectuals, including his friends Ralph Waldo Emerson and Henry David Thoreau.

Concord was already famous as the "Birthplace of the American Revolution" because the first shot of the war between the American colonists and the British was fired at the Old North Bridge over the Concord River. Emerson called it "the shot heard 'round the world." Now, however, Concord was receiving attention as a literary and philosophical center; it was here that the Transcendentalist movement had its roots.

Just as she had explored Boston, Louisa set out to explore Concord. She roamed through the meadows and woods near their cottage, discovering the Concord River that flowed nearby. Walden Pond was only two miles away; the Alcotts often took picnics to its shores in the summertime. There was a new baby sister, too; May was born in 1840, the year after the Alcotts moved to Concord.

After about two years, however, Bronson decided to move his family once again. He wanted to try out some of his new ideas of living in a self-sufficient community. In 1843, they moved twenty miles further west of Concord to a farm they named Fruitlands. Here the Alcotts, along with several other people, planted their own crops, harvested the fruit from the orchards, worked and studied together. Unfortunately, the experiment failed after six months and the Alcotts moved into a boarding house in a nearby town while they decided what they should do next.

Louisa was now eleven years old and her talent for writing was beginning to emerge. She had begun to keep a journal and to write little plays for her sisters and friends to perform. Her mother encouraged

Louisa May Alcott

Louisa in her writing. She set up a family "mailbox" so that they could all write letters and notes to each other every day. This custom was followed in the Alcott home for years and became the inspiration for the "post-office" between the March and Laurence homes in *Little Women.*

In 1844, the Alcotts moved back to Concord and, the next spring, bought a house near the Emerson home. They named it Hillside. During their three years at Hillside, many of the incidents Louisa related in *Little Women* took place—the dramatic plays that Louisa wrote and produced, the short stories she wrote in her garret "hide-away" and submitted to magazines in hopes of publication, and the "Pickwick Club" she and her sisters formed. The girls skated on the Mill Brook nearby, hiked in the hills and woods behind Hillside, went boating on the Concord River, and took picnics to the Great Meadows along the river.

Meanwhile, financial difficulties, always a problem for the Alcotts, continued to shape their lives. Early on, Louisa realized that her father was too much of a dreamer ever to earn much of a living for his family. Her mother had begun to work as a "missionary to the poor" and Louisa decided that she must

Anna Alcott Pratt

do what she could to help, too. When the family left Concord and moved back to Boston, Anna, now seventeen, became a governess, and Louisa kept house for the family, taking in sewing and laundry to help with household expenses. Elizabeth and May went to school.

While Louisa worked at home, she continued to write, for she was convinced that her stories and poems would someday sell. Finally, in 1851, when she was nearly nineteen, *Peterson's Magazine* published her poem "Sunlight." Soon, some of her short stories were published, but Louisa knew that the five or ten dollars she received from these occasional publications would not be enough to help the family as much as she wanted. She found work as a tutor, seamstress, and live-in maid and kept writing when she had time. In 1854, Louisa's first book,* *Flower Fables*, was published. It was a collection of short stories that she had written some years before for Ellen Emerson, Ralph Waldo Emerson's daughter.

Late in 1857, the Alcotts decided to move back to Concord again, where Bronson could be close to his friend Emerson. With the help of Emerson and Abigail's brother, they purchased a house and land next door to their former home, Hillside, now called The Wayside and owned by Nathaniel Hawthorne, author of *The Scarlet Letter* and *The House of the Seven Gables*. The Alcotts' house needed a great deal of work before they could move in, so they lived for the winter months in a little house near the Town Hall in the center of Concord. Their primary concern now, however, was

*Elizabeth
Sewall Alcott*

---

*A recently discovered manuscript entitled *The Inheritance*, written when Louisa was seventeen (1849), was not published in her lifetime.

John Bridge Pratt

Elizabeth. She had never recovered from a debilitating case of scarlet fever and now she was growing weaker every day. In March 1858, at age twenty-three, Elizabeth died in her mother's arms with her father and sisters at her bedside.

Work on the house continued and, in July 1858, the Alcotts moved in. They called it Orchard House and it would be the family home for the next nineteen years. Although Louisa never really liked it (she called it "Apple Slump"), she was to spend a good deal of time there. It was in her room upstairs that she would eventually write *Little Women*.

Two years after the family moved into Orchard House, Anna's wedding was held in the parlour. On May 23, 1860, Anna married John Bridge Pratt, to whom she had been engaged since shortly after Elizabeth's death. Louisa had been living in Boston, where she could earn more money for the family, but now she moved into Orchard House to take care of her parents and May. Bronson was now sixty-one and Abigail sixty. May was twenty, teaching in Concord and studying art.

Meanwhile, war was brewing. Slavery had become the dividing issue between the Northern and Southern states. The Alcotts, staunch abolitionists, had helped runaway slaves to freedom along the Underground Railroad for years. In April 1861, shots were fired at Fort Sumter, South Carolina, and the Civil War began. Louisa spent the first months of the war writing her stories, starting two novels, *Work* and *Moods*, sewing and knitting for the Union soldiers, and keeping house in Concord. But she felt restless and "wanted something to do." In November 1862, Louisa volunteered as a nurse, was accepted, and journeyed to Washington in December. She was a good nurse and the sight of so many sick and wounded young men made an unforgettable impression on her. She worked long hours in poor conditions. After only a few weeks, she became critically ill with typhoid fever and Bronson came to take her back home.

When Louisa recovered, she wrote about her experiences as an Army nurse and submitted the stories, "Hospital Sketches," to the *Boston Commonwealth*; they were very well received and were published as a book that summer. Her writing career had already been boosted a few months earlier when her story "Pauline's Passion and Punishment" won first prize in a contest sponsored by *Frank Leslie's Illustrated Newspaper*. That year she earned $300, and for the first time, her earnings came exclusively from her writing. Although she did not realize it then, Louisa would never again have to resort to teaching or sewing for a living. Louisa spent the rest of the war years writing, keeping house in Con-

The Alcott House

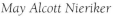
May Alcott Nieriker   *Ernest Nieriker*

cord, and helping raise money for the war effort. Her sister Anna now had two little sons and May was continuing her artwork.

In July 1865, another dream came true for Louisa—she was on her way to Europe! She had been asked to go as a nurse/companion to Anna Weld, the invalid daughter of a Boston shipping merchant. She was gone a year. It was on this trip that she met a young Polish man named Ladislas Wisniewski; they became good friends and Louisa later modeled the character Laurie after him.

In May 1868, Louisa began work on a "girls' story" that had been requested nearly a year before by Thomas Niles, a partner in the Roberts Brothers publishing house. Louisa had resisted the idea, but decided to try. She chose her own family as inspiration—her quiet, scholarly father; her gentle, energetic mother; and the four daughters, each with her own distinct personality.

Once she started the book, she hardly stopped, writing day and night "in a vortex," as she described it. By July, she had finished it. Mr.

Niles thought it "dull" but, after giving it to some girls to read and hearing them pronounce it "splendid," went ahead with publication that fall. *Little Women*, the fictional story of one year in the life of the March family, was a tremendous success and Mr. Niles asked for a sequel for spring publication. Louisa complied and immediately began writing *Little Women*, Part Second, which began with Meg's wedding.

Louisa May Alcott at her desk in Orchard House

For the next twenty years, Louisa May Alcott would continue to write, care for her family, and advocate for women's right to vote, although she had frequent periods of illness. Death began to claim more members of her family—John Pratt in 1870, her mother in 1877, after a long decline, and her sister May in 1879. May was living in Europe and had married Ernest Nieriker in 1878. Just six weeks after giving birth to their daughter, Louisa, she died of meningitis. Bronson was still active in Concord, teaching and writing until 1882 when he suffered a stroke; Anna and Louisa cared for him until his death in 1888.

In September 1880, Louisa met her ten-month-old namesake for the first time. It had been decided that May's baby should come to live with Louisa, so "Lulu" was brought over from France. Louisa was a doting aunt and foster mother to her new "daughter" and spent most of her time with her for the next few years; between caring for Lulu and Bronson, and trying to overcome her own health problems, writing had to take last place. Still, she managed to write *Jo's Boys*, *A Garland for Girls*, and many short stories.

By 1888, Louisa's health had deteriorated completely and she was living in a nursing home near Boston. Her father, who had been moved to Boston, was very near death. Louisa visited him one last time on March 1 and caught a chill driving back home. Bronson died on March 4. Two days later, on March 6, Louisa died at age fifty-five.

The Story of
Little Women and Beyond

LITTLE WOMEN—PART FIRST

Little Women is the story of four girls growing up in a New England village at the start of the Civil War, in 1861. Meg, Jo, Beth, and Amy March struggle with their family's poverty, their own shortcomings, and family illnesses while going to their first dances, making new friends, falling in love, and entertaining themselves with their own plays, or "theatricals," summer picnics, winter skating, and all sorts of other amusements.

Through all of their joys and trials, their beloved Marmee guides them with her gentle and wise counsel, and their father, who is away at war during most of that year, provides inspiration in his letters home.

We are introduced to the March girls on Christmas Eve and, right away, we "know" them . . .

THE MARCH FAMILY TREE

Mrs. March
1815–1885

Mr. March
b. 1814

m. c. 1843

Meg
b. 1844

John Brooke
d. 1876

m. 1865

Friedrich Bhaer
b. 1826

Jo
b. 1845

m. 1870

Beth
1847–1868

Theodore Laurence
b. 1845

Amy
b. 1848

m. 1870

Daisy
b. 1866

Demi
b. 1866

Rob
b. 1871

Teddy
b. 1874

Bess
b. 1871

Josie
b. 1872

• Jo •

"Christmas won't be Christmas without any presents," grumbled
Jo, lying on the rug.

—Little Women, *Chapter One*

Jo, short for Josephine, speaks her mind and refuses to sugarcoat her feelings. She seems to enjoy shocking people a bit—her manners, her way of dressing, and her language are unconventional. She is a "tomboy," for no ladylike fifteen-year-old girl of the day would dream of "lying on the rug." Soon we learn she uses slang, puts her hands in her pockets, whistles, and wishes she had been born a boy.

To help earn some money for the family, Jo goes every day to Aunt March's house to keep her company, run errands, and read to her. Aunt March's library, full of books, Jo's first love, is the main attraction; Jo secretly hopes that Aunt March may one day ask her to accompany her on a trip to Europe.

Jo's dearest ambition is to be a writer and she spends much of her spare time at her little desk in the garret, "scribbling" stories, and sending them off to magazine editors.

• Meg •

"It's so dreadful to be poor!" sighed Meg, looking down at her
old dress.

—Little Women, *Chapter One*

Meg, the eldest at sixteen, is much more conventional than Jo and is the "second mother" to the girls when Marmee is away. She tries her best to overcome her disappointment in being poor but finds it difficult not to have pretty clothes and go to parties as her friends are doing. She is very concerned about good manners and is constantly trying to reform Jo, or at least talk her into observing a few "refinements" such as taking short steps instead of long strides and not shaking hands with people when they are introduced—"It isn't the thing," she says.

Meg is a governess to the King children in town.

• Amy •

"I don't think it's fair for some girls to have plenty of pretty things, and other girls nothing at all," added little Amy, with an injured sniff.

—Little Women, *Chapter One*

The youngest of the girls, Amy is indulged and, at twelve, in danger of being "spoiled." She is self-centered and inclined to be "rather conceited." She is, however, quite a talented artist and experiments with drawing, painting, sculpting, even wood-burning. She is still in school but, after her teacher discovers her with two dozen forbidden pickled limes in her desk and punishes her severely, she leaves school, refusing to return.

• Beth •

"We've got father and mother and each other," said Beth contentedly, from her corner.

—Little Women, *Chapter One*

Beth is considered the angel of the family. She is tenderhearted and shy, so shy that she hardly ventures away from home. She studies her lessons at home, helps with the housekeeping, and is kept busy with her "doll hospital," for she cannot bear to see her dolls or her sisters' discarded just because they are old or ugly or worn out. She is thirteen and loves music more than anything, coaxing music out of the old piano to accompany the songs they all sing together before going to bed.

On Christmas Eve, a letter from their father inspires the girls to try harder to overcome their problems and work toward becoming the "little women" of whom he is already so fond and so proud. Marmee reminds them of their old childhood game of acting out their favorite book, *The Pilgrim's Progress.* Like the hero of that book, the little girls would carry their "burdens" (really Marmee's "piece-bags") on their backs along the "pathway of life" from the City of Destruction (the cellar of the house) to the Celestial City (the flat roof full of flowers and sunshine), trying to avoid such dangers as the fierce lions guarding the "Palace Called Beautiful,' fighting the monster Apollyon, resisting the temptations of "Vanity Fair," and passing through the "Valley of the Shadow" along the way.

This "game," now to be played in earnest, is the framework for *Little Women.* Marmee explains that their "burdens" are the personal flaws they are trying to overcome and "longing for goodness and happiness is the guide that leads us through many troubles and mistakes to the peace which is a true Celestial City."

One of the most satisfying events of their year is finally becoming friends with Laurie, the grandson of the wealthy Mr. Laurence next door, and then with Mr. Laurence himself. The gulf between the poor-but-happy Marches and the rich-but-somewhat-unhappy Laurences is dramatic, but quickly bridged once they begin to know one another. Mr. Laurence finds ways to help the Marches without injuring their pride— he sends them a Christmas supper when he learns they have given away their breakfast to the poor Hummel family and he gives Beth a new piano when he discovers her love of music.

Laurie and Jo become friends at once and soon Laurie is part of the March sisters' close-knit circle. They invite him to become a member of their Pickwick Club and he fixes up a private post office box for the two families to exchange gifts and messages. Meanwhile, Meg is becoming aware of Laurie's tutor, John Brooke, and they begin to fall in love, much to Jo's horror.

When Marmee is suddenly called to Washington to care for Mr.

March, who is ill, the girls are left at home in the care of their longtime housekeeper, Hannah. They all do their best to carry on as usual, but one day, Beth falls ill with scarlet fever. Amy is sent to live with Aunt March while Meg, Jo, and Hannah care for Beth. It is a serious case, however, and Beth nearly dies before Marmee can rush home from Washington.

Christmas comes again for the Marches and the best gift of all is the surprise return of their father, who is brought home by John Brooke. John declares his love for Meg and, though she had decided that she is "too young to enter into any engagement at present," she soon changes her mind when Aunt March arrives and threatens to disinherit Meg if she marries John. The happy family gathers for tea, congratulations, and planning the couple's future.

LITTLE WOMEN—PART SECOND

Three years have passed. The Civil War has ended a few weeks earlier and it is now time for Meg and John's wedding. They are married in the parlour with the family and close friends attending. Soon they are settled in their cottage nearby, which Laurie calls the "Dove-cote," and Meg enthusiastically begins her career as homemaker and, a year later, mother of twins Daisy and Demi.

Amy, who has made much progress in lightening her "burdens" of selfishness and vanity over the last three years, means to become "a true gentlewoman in mind and manners," hoping to rise above "the little meannesses and follies and faults that spoil so many women." She is rewarded for her efforts with the offer of a trip to Europe with Aunt Carrol and her daughter Flo, much to Jo's disappointment, for she had wanted to be chosen.

Jo's outrageous behavior costs her the tour of Europe she has long hoped for: in one reckless moment, Jo implies to Aunt Carrol that she would not want to travel as a "companion" and could not be bothered with learning a foreign language. Of course, Aunt Carrol determines that Jo would not be a suitable traveling companion on her upcoming trip to Europe. Jo stays at home with her parents and Beth for a few months, then decides to go to New York for the winter to tutor the Kirke children, to get new ideas for her stories, and to escape from Laurie, whom she feels is "getting too fond" of her. She meets Friedrich Bhaer, a professor from Germany, and they become friends.

When Jo returns home in the spring, she finds that Beth, who never fully regained her strength after the scarlet fever she had four years before, has grown noticeably worse. Jo determines not to leave her again and stays at home to help care for her.

Meanwhile, Laurie has declared his love for Jo and tries his best to convince her to marry him. She refuses, however, knowing that, while they make the best of friends, they would not have a satisfactory marriage. Laurie does not accept the truth gracefully and sails off to Europe to soothe his feelings. There, he and Amy meet and, after many months, find that they have fallen in love.

Beth weakens day by day during the winter and, finally, in the dawn of a spring morning, draws her last breath. Heartbroken but comforted that she is "well at last," the Marches say good-bye to their "household saint."

Amy and Laurie return home in November and, to everyone's surprise and delight, announce that they are now "Mr. and Mrs. Laurence." The celebration continues into the evening when another surprise guest arrives—Professor Bhaer has come to town and has stopped by to see his friend "Miss Marsch." He stays in town two weeks, visiting the Marches—and Jo—every day. Suddenly, his visits stop and Jo goes to town in search of him. They meet and, on the walk back home in the pouring rain, reveal their love for each other.

The professor and Jo marry and start a "school for boys" in the huge old house that Aunt March has left Jo in her will. The school thrives and, as the book ends, the whole family and the Plumfield boys gather to celebrate Marmee's sixtieth birthday with a day of fun and games and an outdoor picnic in the apple orchard. Marmee gathers her three daughters close and, nearly overcome with the joy of being together, exclaims—

"O my girls, however long you may live, I never can wish you a greater happiness than this!"

LITTLE MEN

Jo and Professor Bhaer's School for Boys is well established now at Plumfield. The twelve boys study their lessons with Professor Bhaer, are cared for by Jo, Asia the cook, and Nursey Hummel. They have garden plots, help with the work around the school, and are encouraged to develop their own unique talents. Jo decides to add girls to her school and Daisy, Meg's ten-year-old daughter, and her friend Annie Harding, called "Nan," join the boys at Plumfield.

Many of the people from *Little Women* play a part in helping the school succeed. "Uncle Teddy," as Laurie is called by the boys, helps finance some of the special projects at the school, such as fixing up a nature museum in the old carriage house where the boys can display the treasures they find on their rambles through the fields and woods around Plumfield. Marmee and Father March and Mr. Laurence come often to visit, along with Amy, Meg, and John Brooke.

John Brooke—Meg's patient, kind, and stalwart husband of over ten years—becomes ill and dies unexpectedly, leaving Meg and their children, Daisy, Demi, and little Josie, to the care of the family.

As the book ends, the children of Plumfield celebrate Thanksgiving, with the bounty of their garden crops making up most of the feast. They present a variety of entertainments and then sing a happy song to "Father and Mother Bhaer."

JO'S BOYS

Ten years after the Thanksgiving celebration that ends *Little Men*, we find Jo and Meg reflecting on the changes that have taken place at Plumfield and in their lives. Marmee and Mr. Laurence have died, as have two of the Plumfield boys, Dick and Billy. The others have grown up and started to make their own way in business, medicine, law, music, journalism, and other occupations. They return to Plumfield from time to time to see their old friends.

Plumfield has grown into a little community where Jo, Meg, Amy, and their families live and work together. Mr. Laurence has endowed a college that has been built nearby, with Professor Bhaer and Mr. March in charge. Amy and Laurie have built a home on a hill just beyond Plumfield that everyone calls "Mount Parnassus" because so many artists are encouraged to come there to study and work. A replica of the Brookes' cottage, the Dove-cote, has been built on the grounds of Plumfield for Meg to live in.

Jo has just written a best-selling book and is now a famous author who is the object of much public adoration and curiosity. She now must try to balance the requests for autographs and pictures with time for her new writing projects.

Some of the Plumfield boys have already married, but there are a few romances still budding—Demi is interested in Alice Heath, a student at Laurence College; Dan Kean has returned after a long and mysterious absence and falls in love with Bess, Amy and Laurie's beautiful daughter; and Nat Blake must prove his success as a violinist before Meg will allow her Daisy to consider him a suitor.

Before the book ends, we learn the histories and the fates of Jo's "little men" and then, "the curtain falls forever on the March family."

The World of
Orchard House

A History of
Orchard House

The Alcotts lived at many addresses over the years, but Orchard House was the home in which they lived the longest—nineteen years. It is also where Louisa May Alcott wrote her best-known book, *Little Women*. Even though Louisa and her sisters did not grow up at Orchard House, she used it as a model for the March family house in *Little Women* with a few features added from her memories of some of her other childhood homes.

When purchased by the Alcotts in 1857 for $950, Orchard House consisted of just four rooms. It was situated on twelve acres of land about a mile east of the village of Concord.

The new property gave Bronson Alcott, a talented, if untrained, architect and landscape designer, a great deal to work with. The main house was small and needed considerable remodeling. There were already mature apple trees on the land and Bronson looked forward to planting more of those as well as other fruit trees and kitchen crops.

The
Laurences'
House

Lexington Road

Built in about 1700, perhaps as early as 1672, Orchard House began as a typical New England house. There were two rooms downstairs and two rooms upstairs. There was also a "tenant house" on the property, built early in the eighteenth century. Bronson had that house moved and added on to the rear of the main house; its rooms became the dining room and kitchen downstairs and two small bedrooms upstairs. He reconfigured the main staircase and added a front porch and a woodshed, which included a bathing room and a workshop. Over the years, there would be more additions and modifications.

Bronson was rather innovative and designed several conveniences for the new house. He built the woodshed door and other utility doors with slightly slanted tops so that they would close automatically, an important feature in the frigid New England winters. He also built in a special water heater behind the kitchen stove and a folding clothes-drying rack on the kitchen wall. He designed a half-moon desk for Louisa's room upstairs so that she would have the light from two windows while she wrote.

The furnishings in Orchard House were somewhat plain, especially compared to the fashionable furniture of the period, which was very heavy and ornately carved, with bright velvet upholstery. The Alcotts preferred simpler pieces from the early nineteenth century. Sofas and chairs were upholstered mostly in black horsehair.

The east parlour and the dining room just behind it were the rooms Mrs. Alcott (Marmee in *Little Women*) and her daughters spent the most time in. The light in the parlour was good for sewing and reading and the room was comfortably furnished with a sofa (complete with a "sausage" pillow just like Jo's) and several chairs, needlepoint-covered "footwarmers" (little footstools that could be filled with coals from the fireplace), and pictures on the walls painted by May (Amy in *Little Women*). A piano, given to the Alcotts by one of Mrs. Alcott's relatives, stood in one corner. A double-wide doorway, hung with heavy draperies, led to the dining room that occasionally served as a staging area for Louisa's plays. In the dining room, the Alcotts kept Elizabeth's little "melodeon" (a small piano-like instrument), even though she was no longer there to play it. Elizabeth (Beth) never lived at Orchard House; she died four months before the family moved in.

The kitchen was behind the dining room. There was a covered porch on one side, and a large woodshed on the other so that wood could be fetched for the stove and fireplaces without anyone's having to go outside. The well was outside, behind the kitchen.

The west parlour was Bronson Alcott's study. Behind it was a lean-to room that May used as a studio; later this was remodeled and used as a breakfast room.

Bedrooms were upstairs. Anna and Louisa (Jo) shared the east front room. It was furnished with a large sleigh bed, nightstand, bureau, a

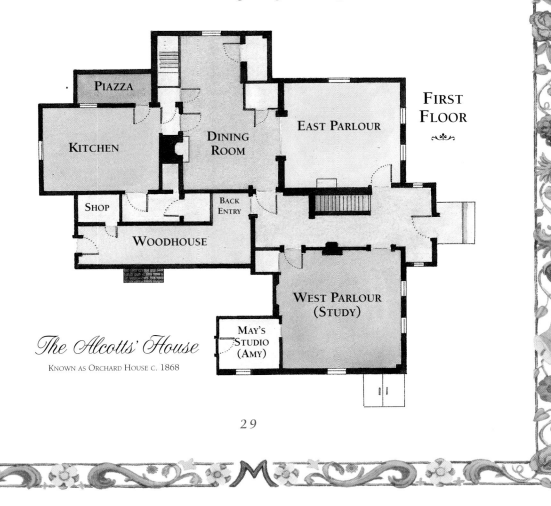

FIRST FLOOR

PIAZZA

EAST PARLOUR

KITCHEN

DINING ROOM

SHOP

BACK ENTRY

WOODHOUSE

WEST PARLOUR (STUDY)

MAY'S STUDIO (AMY)

The Alcotts' House

KNOWN AS ORCHARD HOUSE C. 1868

large round table, desk and chair, and built-in bookcases. Anna lived at Orchard House for two years before she was married to John Pratt (John Brooke) in the east parlour in May 1860 and they moved to Boston. Louisa spent most of those first two years in Boston, working and writing, but after Anna married, Louisa moved into Orchard House to help with the housekeeping.

There was a large fireplace in Louisa's bedroom that May decorated with a painting of an owl in Louisa's honor—she called Louisa their "wise owl." In 1863, while Louisa was recovering from typhoid fever in her room at Orchard House, May also painted a beautiful wall panel of calla lilies and nasturtiums on one side of the half-moon desk. In the summer of 1868, Louisa wrote *Little Women* here.

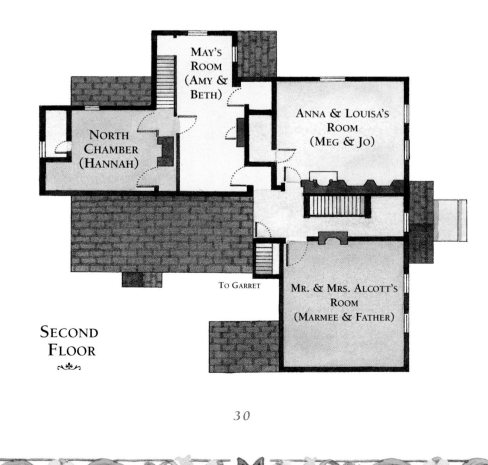

MAY'S ROOM (AMY & BETH)

NORTH CHAMBER (HANNAH)

ANNA & LOUISA'S ROOM (MEG & JO)

TO GARRET

MR. & MRS. ALCOTT'S ROOM (MARMEE & FATHER)

SECOND FLOOR

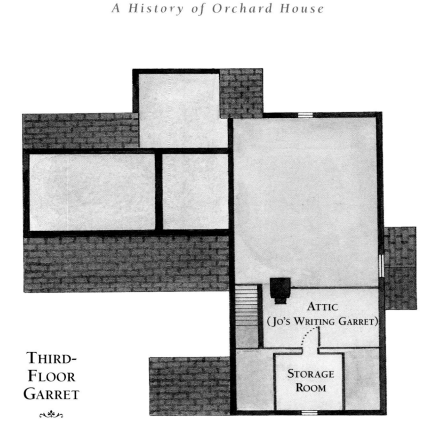

**THIRD-
FLOOR
GARRET**

ATTIC
(Jo's Writing Garret)

STORAGE
ROOM

May's room was behind Louisa's room, over the dining room. It was furnished with blue-and-white "cottage" furniture that she herself may have painted with ribbons and floral bouquets. She decorated the walls and doors with her own drawings and sketches. There was a tiny staircase that led from May's room down to the dining room—very handy for costume changes when the Alcotts gave their plays and theatricals.

Behind May's room was the north chamber, designated as a servant's room. There is no record of the Alcotts' having live-in servants during the years before Louisa wrote *Little Women*, but she must have had this room in mind for Hannah, the indispensable housekeeper for the March family.

The master bedroom was at the front of the house across from Louisa's room. It was furnished simply with a bed and bureaus, a washstand from the May family, chairs and worktable, and quilts made by Mrs. Alcott.

As the years went by, Bronson added more bedrooms upstairs for Anna and her sons, who moved back into Orchard House after John Pratt died in 1870. He also remodeled his study and added more sheds to the back of the house for storage.

There were orchards on both sides of the house, a kitchen garden, a rose terrace, and many large hardwood trees and evergreens. Paths led from the house up the steep hill behind it and from the front of the house through the woods to the Hawthorne house. Bronson also designed and built a rustic "summer-house" (gazebo) behind the main house.

In 1877, after nineteen years at Orchard House, the Alcotts bought the Thoreau house in Concord and moved there, while renting out Orchard House for a number of years. In 1879, Bronson arranged to conduct a school in his old study at Orchard House and then, in 1880, erected a little building for his School of Philosophy where the summerhouse had been. The Alcotts sold Orchard House in 1884.

At the turn of the century, Orchard House was bought by Harriet Lothrop, who wrote *The Five Little Peppers* series under the name of Margaret Sidney. She believed the house should be preserved as a memorial to the Alcotts; thus, in 1911, the Louisa May Alcott Memorial Association was formed and Orchard House was opened for public visits. Furnished largely with original Alcott pieces, it continues to receive thousands of visitors every year.

For more information, write to

Orchard House
Box 343
Concord, Massachusetts 01742

Fruitlands, the site of the Alcotts' farm near Harvard, Massachusetts, is open to visitors as well. For more information, write to

Fruitlands Museums
102 Prospect Hill Road
Harvard, Massachusetts 01451

The Wayside, the Alcott-Hawthorne house, now a part of the National Park Service's Minute Man National Historical Park in Concord, is also open to visitors. For more information, write to

Minute Man National Historical Park
174 Liberty Street
Concord, Massachusetts 01742

Other Alcott-related sites to visit in Concord include Ralph Waldo Emerson's home, near Orchard House; Sleepy Hollow Cemetery, where the Alcott family and other Concord notables are buried; Walden Pond and Walden Woods, where Henry David Thoreau lived and where the Alcotts often picnicked with friends. The Thoreau-Alcott house on Main Street in Concord is privately owned and not open to the public. The cottage in town where Elizabeth Alcott died is no longer standing. The "Laurence House" and "Plumfield," while loosely based on houses Louisa knew in other places, did not exist in Concord.

The
Palace Beautiful

Daily Life in the
Little Women Era

"The Dustpan Society will meet on Wednesday next and parade in the upper story of the Club House. All members to appear and shoulder their brooms at nine precisely."
—From The Pickwick Portfolio, Little Women, *Chapter Ten*

In the March girls' favorite book, *The Pilgrim's Progress*, one of the stops on Christian's journey to the Celestial City was "The Palace called 'Beautiful.' " It stood by the side of the road and had been built "for the relief and security of pilgrims." What better description could be found for the March home? Meg, Jo, Beth, and Amy considered themselves pilgrims, carrying their burdens of vanity, pride, bashfulness, and selfishness on their own journeys to the Celestial City. Their "Palace Beautiful" was not fashionable or elegant—it was furnished largely with secondhand furniture and homemade accessories—but it was always their "relief and security," because there they found a loving family and devoted friends.

Next door to the Marches was another "Palace Beautiful," the home of the Laurences. A "stately stone mansion," it was Jo's idea of an "enchanted palace, full of splendors and delights." But it was "lonely and lifeless," inhabited only by old Mr. Laurence, his grandson Laurie, and a staff of servants. The servants cleaned, cooked, took care of the gardens, and kept the estate in perfect order.

In the March household, the domestic life was quite different. Their only servant was Hannah Mullet and she was more "a friend than a servant." Hannah had lived with the Marches since Meg was a baby and, although she took charge of the cooking and major housekeeping duties, Marmee and all of the girls helped, for in the days before electric appliances, there was always plenty of work. Marmee discussed sharing these duties with the girls in Chapter Eleven:

> "Don't you feel that it is pleasanter to help one another, to have daily duties which make leisure sweet when it comes, and to bear and forbear, that home may be comfortable and lovely to us all?"

A chart of "Indoor Duties for Children" was used in the Alcott household and we can assume that the Marches followed a similar routine. The family rose at five o'clock in the morning and, after breakfast at six o'clock, the children spent about two hours doing light chores. They studied their lessons for the rest of the morning, and rested for an hour after their dinner at noon. The afternoons were given to sewing, reading, errands, more chores, and "recreations" such as writing and performing plays, and hiking up the ridge in back of the house that the girls called "Delectable Mountain" after another *Pilgrim's Progress* site. Supper was at six o'clock and bedtime was usually at eight or eight-thirty (nine o'clock when the girls were older).

Most of the March girls' work involved sewing, mending, and embroidery, but they were also responsible for other light chores—dusting, airing the rooms, arranging flowers, and keeping things neat. When Marmee was called to Washington to care for Mr. March, all of the girls

The Alcotts' household duties chart

added more housekeeping duties to their daily schedule. "Hope and keep busy" was their motto during those anxious weeks.

"Keeping busy" meant a good deal of hard work. Wood had to be chopped and brought in to keep the fireplaces and cookstove constantly replenished; the fireplaces and cookstove also had to be cleaned out regularly. Ashes were shoveled into tin buckets and saved for making soap or sprinkled on the gardens for fertilizer. Water for cooking, washing, and bathing had to be brought in from the well or a rain barrel and heated on the kitchen stove. (The Alcotts did not have indoor water until the 1870s.)

There were lighter daily tasks, too. Lamps had to be kept filled with kerosene, their wicks trimmed and glass chimneys cleaned of soot. Three meals a day had to be prepared and the dishes washed afterward. The floors were swept and the furniture was dusted each day as there were no window screens to keep insects or leaves from blowing in, and fireplaces created fine ash and soot that settled on everything.

Doing the laundry was one of the biggest tasks of the household. It was usually begun early on Monday morning with the hauling in of many pails of water, which were poured into a large pot on the kitchen stove. When the water was hot, shavings from a large bar of soap were dropped in; then the white clothes or linens were stirred into the hot, soapy water with a long stick. They were "cooked" and stirred for about a half hour, then lifted out of the water with the stick and put into an empty tub and drained. The heavy pot of soapy water was carried outside and emptied; fresh water was brought in and heated to rinse the clothes. The entire process was repeated for colored clothes. If the clothes were especially dirty, they had to be scrubbed on a washboard. After the final rinse, the cottons and linens were dipped in starch; this added body and a glossy finish to the cloth and made ironing easier.

After the clothes were rinsed, starched, and squeezed as dry as possible, they were hung up to dry. In warm, sunny weather, they were hung on a line outside. But in cold, wet weather, they were hung up indoors—in the kitchen, the cellar, or the attic.

Once the clothes were dry, it was time to iron them. Heavy flatirons were heated on the kitchen stove and, when water that was dripped on them sizzled, they were hot enough to press the clothes. When an iron cooled down, it was put back on the stove to reheat; another hot iron from the stove was taken up to continue the ironing. To keep starch in the clothes from sticking to the irons, a cloth bag of beeswax was kept nearby and rubbed lightly over the bottom of the iron just before it was used; before the iron was put back on the stove, it was rubbed with a piece of sandpaper to remove any starch that might be sticking to it.

Various seasons presented special tasks. Late summer and fall meant drying and preserving as many fruits and vegetables as possible. Apples, potatoes, carrots, parsnips, and onions were stored in the cellar; berries and other fruits were made into preserves, jams, or jellies; beans and peas were dried and stored in jars or covered metal cans; cucumbers and other vegetables were pickled. Herbs were gathered from the garden and hung in bunches to dry. Living only a mile from town, the Marches could go to the markets for meats, flour, sugar, tea, coffee, and other items.

After a long winter when the fires in the fireplaces had been burning all day, every day, creating a smoky film over walls and furnishings, it was time to clean the entire house. Rugs were carried outside, hung on the clothesline, and struck with wire or rattan "rug beaters" until there was not a speck of dust or dirt remaining in them. Floors were mopped and waxed. Walls, ceilings, woodwork, and windows were washed; fresh whitewash was applied to the kitchen walls. Curtains and bedclothes were laundered. The cellar was cleaned and disinfected, the attic swept and dusted. Fireplaces were cleaned and covered with "fireboards"—wooden panels cut to fit the fireplace openings and painted to add a decorative touch to the room for the summer months.

Meg was especially talented at traditional household activities—Hannah wrote to Marmee that "Miss Meg is going to make a proper good housekeeper; she hes the liking for it, and gits the hang of things surprisin' quick." Beth was "a sight of help" to Hannah, too, taking charge of the marketing and keeping the household accounts. But Amy and Jo were not quite as gifted in domestic endeavors, being more interested in their artistic and literary pursuits. Even so, Jo was energetic—"Jo doos beat all for goin ahead, but she don't stop to cal'k'late fust . . . ," Hannah wrote after Jo had tried to help Hannah with the laundering but starched the clothes *before* rinsing them and "blued a pink calico dress" (bluing was supposed to be added only to white clothes to keep them from turning gray and dull). As the youngest, most indulged of the sisters, Amy seems not to have been expected to do as much housework. Nonetheless, Marmee's instructions to her before leaving for Washington were "help all you can, be obedient, and keep happy safe at home"—advice all the March girls heeded during her absence.

The Wide, Wide World

Little Women Treasury
Time Line

1860–1888

I n a careful reading of *Little Women*, *Little Men*, and *Jo's Boys*, we can tell what year certain events in the stories took place, even though the stories themselves are fiction.

Little Women, Part First, of course, is set during the Civil War, which took place from April 1861 to April 1865. In Chapter Nineteen, we are given the only firm date in the series when Amy writes her "will" and dates it November 20, 1861. Although this is the date from which we calculate all the other dates for the characters and events in the series, it also creates a bit of confusion. Louisa begins *Little Women* in the previous December, which would have to be 1860. This was four months before the war actually started; yet Louisa had Mr. March and "our men" already "fighting" and "suffering so in the Army." Nevertheless, we begin our time line with 1860, based on the date of Amy's will.

Meg, we are told in Chapter One, is sixteen, Jo, fifteen, Beth, thirteen, and Amy, twelve. Laurie says at the New Year's Eve party that he will be "Sixteen, next month." A few simple calculations, deducting the ages of each girl and Laurie from 1860, give us the year each was born (see the March Family Tree, page 14). Part First of *Little Women* ends in December 1861 with Mr. March's return and Meg's engagement to John Brooke.

Little Women, Part Second, begins three and a half years later, when "the war is over," which would be 1865. Meg is about to be married. Louisa's sister Anna (Meg in *Little Women*) was married on May 23 (in 1860, not in 1865) and this is probably the day Louisa had in mind for Meg's wedding, since most of the other details of Meg's wedding are exactly as Louisa, and others, had described Anna's.

There are clues to other dates as well. In the last chapter of *Little Women*, Jo says she is thirty and Marmee is sixty; since we have already been able to establish Jo's birth year as 1845, this would mean that *Little Women* ended in 1875. From this date, we can subtract sixty and arrive at Marmee's birth year—1815. In *Little Men*, we learn that Demi is " 'most ten" (he and Daisy were born in 1866, a year after Meg and John were married), so we know that *Little Men* is set in the year 1876, from spring to Thanksgiving in late November. In *Jo's Boys*, we are told that ten years have gone by since *Little Men* ended; since *Jo's Boys* begins in the spring, the year could be 1886 (nine and a half years later, " 'most ten," as Demi might say) or 1887 (ten and a half years later). Since Louisa wrote *Little Men* in 1886, we have chosen that year as the one in which the story begins. The book ends two years later, in March 1888 (coincidentally, this was also the month and year that Louisa died). Thus, after some arithmetic, we have concluded that the series covered the years 1860 to 1888.

In this chapter, you will discover when the different incidents in the *Little Women* series took place and also what *real* events were happening at the same time in the world, including the significant events in Louisa May Alcott's own life.

1860

The March girls—Meg, Jo, Beth, and Amy—prepare for Christmas with their father away in the army. Meg and Jo are invited to Mrs. Gardiner's New Year's Eve dance and meet Laurie, the young man who has come to live with his grandfather next door to the Marches.

Professor Bhaer's nephew, Franz Hoffmann, is born.

- **Abraham Lincoln** is elected sixteenth president of the United States
- South Carolina is the first state to secede from the Union
- The Pony Express begins mail delivery from St. Louis, Missouri, and Sacramento, California
- J. M. Barrie, author of *Peter Pan*, and George Eliot, author of *Silas Marner*, are born
- Cork linoleum and the **typewriter** are invented
- Nathaniel Hawthorne begins remodeling Hillside, former home of the Alcotts next door to Orchard House; Hawthorne had renamed the house The Wayside
- Elizabeth Peabody, friend of the Alcotts and Bronson's assistant in 1834 in the Temple School in Boston, opens her "kindergarten," the first in the United States
  - **Louisa May Alcott** is twenty-eight years old
  - Louisa's sister Anna (prototype for Meg in *Little Women*) is married to John Bridge Pratt at Orchard House
  - **Harriet Tubman** and John Brown's widow and daughters visit the Alcott home

1861

The Marches and the Laurences become fast friends. Mr. Laurence gives Beth a new piano. Amy is humiliated at school over her possession of pickled limes. Amy vengefully throws Jo's manuscript into the fire and, after vowing never to forgive Amy, Jo saves her from drowning. The Pickwick Club and the March-Laurence "post-office" are begun. Mr. March is wounded in the war and Marmee must travel to Washington to care for him; Jo sells her long hair to help pay for the trip. Beth falls ill with scarlet fever and Marmee returns to care for her. Mr. March surprises the family by coming home on Christmas Day. Meg and John Brooke are engaged.

Dan Kean, one of Jo's "little men," is born.

- **The Civil War** begins when Southern soldiers fire on Fort Sumter in the Charleston, South Carolina, harbor, and Union troops surrender
- Union troops are defeated at the Battle of Bull Run
- Elizabeth Barrett Browning, author of the sonnet "How Do I Love Thee," dies in Italy
- Louisa is writing, sewing, and teaching kindergarten in Concord. Her short story, "Pauline's Passion and Punishment," wins first prize of $100 in *Frank Leslie's Illustrated Newspaper* contest.

1862

Ned Barker, one of Jo's "little men," is born.

- **General Robert E. Lee** becomes commander of the Confederate Army
- The Union Army is defeated at Fredericksburg, Virginia
- Julia Ward Howe's "The Battle Hymn of the Republic" is published

- President Lincoln signs the Homestead Act
- Sioux uprising in Minnesota leads to Minnesota Massacre
- **The Union Pacific Railroad** is chartered
- Edith Wharton, author of *The Age of Innocence*, is born
- O. Henry (William Sydney Porter), author of "The Gift of the Magi," is born
  - **Henry David Thoreau**, friend of the Alcott family, dies
  - Louisa goes to Washington as a volunteer nurse to care for wounded soldiers. Clara Barton, who later founded the American Red Cross, and Dorothea Dix, pioneer advocate for the mentally ill, are in charge of choosing and training the nurses.

1863

John Brooke joins Union Army and is wounded.
   Billy Ward and Nat Blake, two of Jo's "little men," are born.

- President Lincoln signs the Emancipation Proclamation
- The Battle of Gettysburg is fought; Lincoln delivers his **"Gettysburg Address"**
- General Stonewall Jackson dies
- West Virginia becomes the thirty-fifth state
- Butterick paper dress patterns are introduced
- Gene Stratton Porter, author of *The Girl of the Limberlost*, is born
- "When Johnny Comes Marching Home," a popular Civil War song by L. Lambert, is published
- After little more than one month as a nurse, Louisa is sent home with typhoid. Her long hair is cut to help bring her fever down.
- Her letters and stories about her experiences as a nurse are published as "Hospital Sketches"

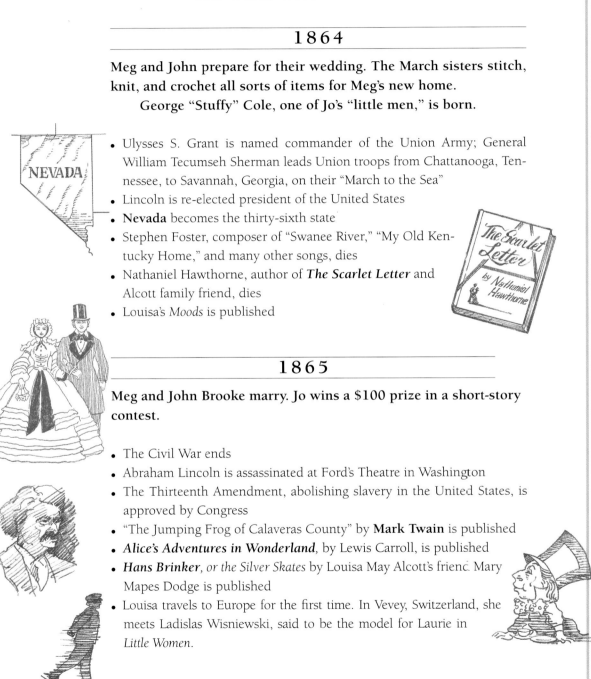

1864

**Meg and John prepare for their wedding. The March sisters stitch, knit, and crochet all sorts of items for Meg's new home.
George "Stuffy" Cole, one of Jo's "little men," is born.**

- Ulysses S. Grant is named commander of the Union Army; General William Tecumseh Sherman leads Union troops from Chattanooga, Tennessee, to Savannah, Georgia, on their "March to the Sea"
- Lincoln is re-elected president of the United States
- **Nevada** becomes the thirty-sixth state
- Stephen Foster, composer of "Swanee River," "My Old Kentucky Home," and many other songs, dies
- Nathaniel Hawthorne, author of **The Scarlet Letter** and Alcott family friend, dies
- Louisa's *Moods* is published

1865

Meg and John Brooke marry. Jo wins a $100 prize in a short-story contest.

- The Civil War ends
- Abraham Lincoln is assassinated at Ford's Theatre in Washington
- The Thirteenth Amendment, abolishing slavery in the United States, is approved by Congress
- "The Jumping Frog of Calaveras County" by **Mark Twain** is published
- **Alice's Adventures in Wonderland,** by Lewis Carroll, is published
- **Hans Brinker,** *or the Silver Skates* by Louisa May Alcott's friend Mary Mapes Dodge is published
- Louisa travels to Europe for the first time. In Vevey, Switzerland, she meets Ladislas Wisniewski, said to be the model for Laurie in *Little Women.*

1866

Twins Daisy and Demi are born to Meg and John. Amy goes to Europe with Aunt Carrol and her daughter Flo; Jo goes to New York to become a governess and she meets Professor Bhaer.

Nan Harding, a future student at Plumfield, is born.

- The Fourteenth Amendment, granting citizenship to African-Americans, is approved by Congress
- Beatrix Potter, author and illustrator of **Peter Rabbit** and other children's stories, is born in England
- Key-opening tin cans are introduced
- Louisa returns to Concord after a year in Europe

1867

Jo returns home from New York in June. Laurie graduates from college; he proposes to Jo and she refuses. Jo realizes that Beth's health is failing.

- **Nebraska** becomes the thirty-seventh state
- The United States purchases Alaska from Russia for $7,200,000
- The Dominion of Canada is established
- **Laura Ingalls Wilder**, author of the *Little House* books, is born
- The ticker-tape machine is invented; the refrigerated railcar is patented
- Publisher Thomas Niles makes his first request to Louisa for "a book for girls"
    - Louisa sees **Charles Dickens**, author of *A Christmas Carol*, on his lecture tour of the United States
    - Louisa accepts a position as editor of *Merry's Museum* magazine. Her annual salary is to be $500.

Beth March

1868

Beth dies in early spring. Amy and Laurie become engaged in Europe. Jo begins to write again and her first novel is published.

Dick Brown and Adolphus "Dolly" Pettingill, two of Jo's "little men," are born.

- Ulysses S. Grant is elected president of the United States
- Bret Harte's "The Luck of Roaring Camp" is published
- The lawn mower, tape measure, and **baseball uniforms** are introduced
- *Little Women,* Part First, is published; Louisa begins writing Part Second

1869

Amy and Laurie are married in Paris; they return home in November. Professor Bhaer comes to visit Jo and proposes. Professor Bhaer leaves for his teaching post in the West. He and Jo "work and wait, hope and love" for a year.

- The Fifteenth Amendment, asserting that no citizen may be denied the right to vote "on account of race, color, or previous condition of servitude," is approved by Congress
- Wyoming Territory gives the vote to women
- The transcontinental railroad is completed
- Austria introduces the first postal cards
- The vacuum cleaner is invented
  - Frank Lloyd Wright, American architect, is born
  - **Little Women, Part Second**, is published
  - May Alcott's book, *Concord Sketches*, is published

1870

Aunt March dies and leaves her home, Plumfield, to Jo. Jo and Professor Bhaer are married and settle at Plumfield, where they start a school for boys.

- General Robert E. Lee dies
- The Standard Oil Company is founded by John D. Rockefeller
- **Charles Dickens**, author of *The Posthumous Papers of the Pickwick Club*, *David Copperfield*, *Oliver Twist*, *A Christmas Carol*, and many other works, dies

  - Jules Verne's *Twenty Thousand Leagues Under the Sea* is published
  - Louisa's *An Old-Fashioned Girl* is published
  - Louisa makes a second trip to Europe
  - John Pratt, husband of Louisa's sister Anna, dies in December

1871

Daisy and Demi are five years old. Jo's first son, Robin, and Amy and Laurie's daughter, Bess, are born.

- Stephen Crane, author of *The Red Badge of Courage*, is born
- **Verdi**'s opera *Aida* debuts
- **Chewing gum** is invented
- *Little Men* is published

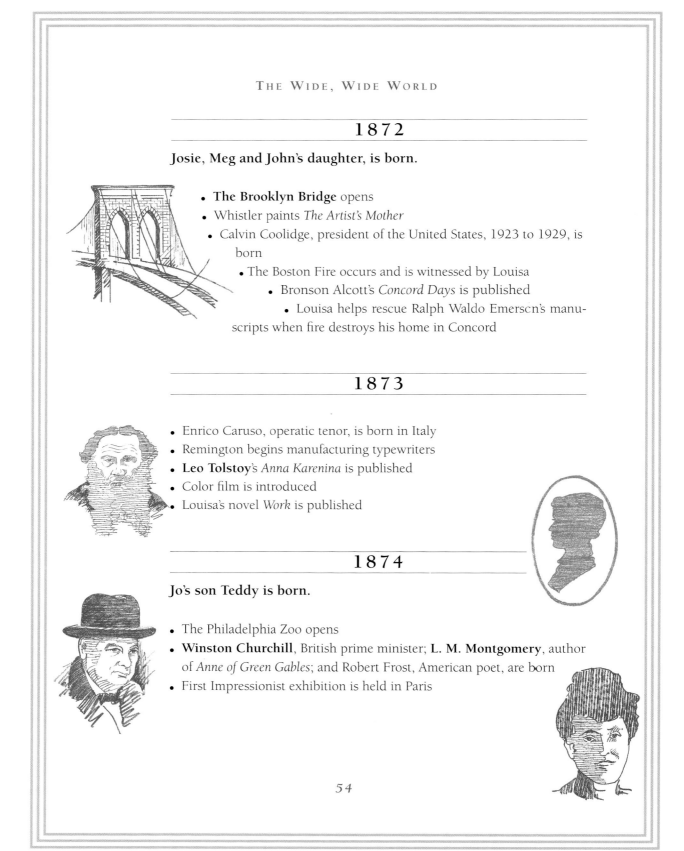

1872

Josie, Meg and John's daughter, is born.

- **The Brooklyn Bridge** opens
- Whistler paints *The Artist's Mother*
- Calvin Coolidge, president of the United States, 1923 to 1929, is born
- The Boston Fire occurs and is witnessed by Louisa
- Bronson Alcott's *Concord Days* is published
- Louisa helps rescue Ralph Waldo Emerson's manuscripts when fire destroys his home in Concord

1873

- Enrico Caruso, operatic tenor, is born in Italy
- Remington begins manufacturing typewriters
- **Leo Tolstoy**'s *Anna Karenina* is published
- Color film is introduced
- Louisa's novel *Work* is published

1874

Jo's son Teddy is born.

- The Philadelphia Zoo opens
- **Winston Churchill**, British prime minister; **L. M. Montgomery**, author of *Anne of Green Gables*; and Robert Frost, American poet, are born
- First Impressionist exhibition is held in Paris

1875

The family gathers for a day of harvesting apples in the Plumfield orchard. They celebrate Marmee's sixtieth birthday.

- Andrew Johnson, successor to President Lincoln, dies
- The Kentucky Derby is run for the first time
- **Bizet**'s opera *Carmen* debuts in Paris
- The baseball glove and football uniforms come into use
- The *Minute Man* statue by Daniel Chester French, a friend of the Alcott family, is dedicated at the Old North Bridge in Concord
- Louisa's *Eight Cousins* is published
- Louisa is the honored guest at the tenth anniversary of Vassar College

1876

Little Men **begins. Nat Blake comes to Plumfield in early spring, joining the twelve boys who are already students there. Demi and Daisy are ten in June. Their father, John Brooke, dies in September.**

- The United States Centennial is celebrated
- Colorado becomes the thirty-eighth state; no more states are added to the Union until 1889, after Louisa's death
- Mark Twain's **Tom Sawyer** is published
  - Jack London, author of *The Call of the Wild*, is born
    - **General George Custer**'s troops are defeated in the Battle of Little Bighorn
    - Alexander Graham Bell patents the telephone
    - Louisa's *Rose in Bloom* is published
      - May Alcott goes to Europe to study art

1877

There is a ten-year gap between *Little Men* and *Jo's Boys* (the years 1876 to 1886). During this decade, Marmee dies. Mr. Laurence also dies and leaves an endowment to build Laurence College near Plumfield. Professor Bhaer becomes its president and Mr. March its chaplain. Jo begins to write again and her "book for girls" becomes an instant success.

- Rutherford B. Hayes is inaugurated president of the United States
- Federal troops are withdrawn from the Southern states
- A Constitutional amendment to permit women to vote is introduced in Congress
- Anna Sewell's *Black Beauty* is published
- Thomas Edison introduces the **phonograph**
- The Alcotts purchase the Thoreau house in Concord and leave Orchard House after living there for nineteen years
- Paris holds its World Exhibition; May Alcott's still life is exhibited with other specially selected paintings (May's painting now hangs in Orchard House)
- Louisa's mother, Abigail May Alcott, dies
- Louisa's *A Modern Mephistopheles* is published

1878

- A malaria epidemic kills thousands of people in Tennessee and Louisiana
- **Bicycles** are manufactured in Europe
- *The Return of the Native* by Thomas Hardy is published
- Louisa's sister May marries Swiss banker Ernest Nieriker in London
- Louisa's *Under the Lilacs* is published

1879

- Mary Baker Eddy, author of *Science and Health*, founds the First Church of Christ, Scientist, in Boston
- E. M. Forster, British author of *Howards End*, *A Room with a View*, and *A Passage to India*, is born
- Henrik Ibsen's *A Doll's House* premieres
- Louisa, escorted by Oliver Wendell Holmes, and Frances Hodgson Burnett, author of *The Secret Garden*, are honored by the Papyrus Club at the Revere House in Boston
- Louisa becomes the first woman in Concord to register to vote
- Bronson Alcott opens his School of Philosophy at Orchard House
- Louisa's sister May dies in Paris, one month after the birth of her daughter, Louisa May ("Lulu") Nieriker

1880

- George Eliot, British author of *Silas Marner*, *Middlemarch*, and other novels, dies in England
- *The Brothers Karamazov* by Feodor Dostoevsky and *Tales from Uncle Remus* by Joel Chandler Harris are published
- Auguste Rodin's sculpture *The Thinker* is completed
- Gilbert and Sullivan's opera *The Pirates of Penzance* is produced
- Cholera vaccine is developed by Louis Pasteur
- Baby Lulu is brought from Paris to live with Louisa
- Louisa's *Jack and Jill* is published

1881

- James A. Garfield is inaugurated president of the United States and assassinated; his vice president, Chester A. Arthur, is sworn in as the twenty-first president
- Chief Sitting Bull surrenders in North Dakota
- **Clara Barton** founds the American Red Cross
- **Robert Louis Stevenson**'s *Treasure Island* is published
- **Pablo Picasso**, painter and sculptor, is born

1882

Nan Harding, once a student at Plumfield, begins medical school at age sixteen. Mr. Laurence dies.

- Henry Wadsworth Longfellow, author of *The Song of Hiawatha,* dies
- Jesse James, notorious bank robber, is killed in Missouri
- **Franklin Delano Roosevelt**, president of the United States from 1933 to 1945, is born
- Samuel Goldwyn, one of the founders of Metro-Goldwyn-Mayer, is born
- **Ralph Waldo Emerson**, friend of the Alcott family and model for Mr. Laurence, dies on April 27
- Bronson Alcott, Louisa's father, has a stroke at age eighty-three
- Louisa's short story "An Old-Fashioned Thanksgiving" is published

1883

- Emma Lazarus composes "The New Colossus: Inscription for the **Statue of Liberty**" for its dedication in New York harbor
- The Metropolitan Opera House in New York City is opened
- The Orient Express, symbol of luxury rail travel, makes its first run from Paris to Istanbul
- Daniel and Harriet ("Margaret Sidney") Lothrop buy The Wayside, known as Hillside when the Alcotts lived there from 1845 to 1848

1884

Marmee dies. Dan visits Plumfield and leaves again for California.

- **The Washington Monument** is completed
- Louisa buys a seaside cottage at Nonquitt
- Orchard House, home to the Alcotts from 1858 to 1877, is sold, having been rented for seven years
- With Louisa and Bronson in declining health, the Alcotts move to Louisburg Square in Boston to be closer to doctors

1885

- **Ulysses S. Grant**, Civil War general and president of the United States, dies
- Anna Pavlova, Russian ballet dancer, is born
- Alexander Graham Bell founds The American **Telephone** and Telegraph Company

1886

Jo's Boys begins. The older Plumfield boys have left to begin careers but return from time to time to visit. When *Jo's Boys* opens in the summer of 1886, we learn that Franz has gone back to Germany to become a merchant and Emil has fulfilled his dream of becoming a sailor. Dan has pursued adventure in South America, Australia, and California. Jack has gone into business; Demi has graduated from college and is beginning a career in journalism. Tom, Dolly, Stuffy, Ned, and Rob are in various stages at college and Nat is finishing his music studies at the Conservatory. Billy and Dick have died.

Of the Plumfield girls, we learn that "Nan began to study medicine at sixteen," Josie and Bess are still in school, and Daisy lives at home with her mother, Meg.

As *Jo's Boys* opens, Emil arrives at Plumfield for a visit between ocean voyages and Dan, having been out West for two years, returns. Over the next few weeks, many of the old Plumfield crowd return for visiting and good times together. In August, Emil's ship sails again, Dan leaves for Kansas, and Nat departs for Germany, where he will study music for a year or two.

Before Thanksgiving, Emil's ship burns at sea and he is believed to have died. Meanwhile, Dan is caught up in a fight, accidentally kills a man, and is charged with manslaughter. He begins to serve a year in prison.

- Pasteur Institute is founded in Paris
- Ty Cobb, baseball player, is born
- Henry James's *The Bostonians* is published
- Louisa's *Jo's Boys* is published

1887

After long weeks of expecting the worst, the Bhaers receive word that Emil is safe. He and Franz return to Plumfield in June, both married. Demi becomes engaged to Alice Heath. In September, Dan is released from prison and, in October, saves twenty men's lives in a mine cave-in. Ted and Laurie go out West to bring him back to Plumfield to recuperate.

- **Queen Victoria**'s Golden Jubilee is celebrated
- Louisa's *A Garland for Girls* is published
- Louisa adopts her nephew John Pratt so that he can inherit her copyrights
- Louisa enters a nursing home in Roxbury, Massachusetts

1888

Nat returns to Plumfield in March and he and Daisy are engaged.

- Benjamin Harrison is elected president of the United States
- T. S. Eliot, poet and winner of the 1948 Nobel Prize for Literature, is born
- Irving Berlin, composer, is born
- Bronson Alcott dies on March 4 at age eighty-eight
- **Louisa** dies on March 6 at age fifty-five

Tea with the
March Family

Recipes from the
Little Women Books

*It was fortunate that tea was at hand, to produce a lull and
provide refreshment . . .* —Little Women, *Chapter Forty-three*

"Tea" for the Marches was their evening meal, a light supper
served with pots of hot tea.

Despite the Boston Tea Party, which occurred in
1773 in Boston Harbor, just twenty miles from the Marches' home in
Concord, Massachusetts, tea remained a favorite beverage of Americans.
During the nineteenth century, most people drank it at every meal.

In this chapter you will learn not only how to make a pot of tea
Little Women style, but also how to make some of the treats that Meg, Jo,
Beth, and Amy enjoyed with their tea.

Hannah's Pot of Tea

. . . the faint sound of a bell warned them that Hannah had put the tea "to draw," and they would just have time to get home to supper. —Little Women, *Chapter Thirteen*

Putting the tea "to draw" meant that Hannah had just poured the boiling water into the teapot and stirred in the tea leaves; the March girls, having spent the afternoon on the hill they called "Delectable Mountain," knew they had about five minutes to get home, for the tea would then be ready to pour.

In 1856, Louisa May Alcott's mother, who was the inspiration for Marmee in *Little Women*, put this recipe for making tea in her small leather-covered "receipt" (recipe) book. Hannah surely used the same method when she made tea for the March family.

The proper way to make a cup of good tea, is a matter of some importance. The teapot is at once filled up with boiling water; then the tea is put into the pot, and is allowed to stand five minutes before it is used. The leaves gradually absorb the water, and as gradually sink to the bottom. The result is, that the tea leaves are not scalded, as they are when boiling water is poured over them, and you get all the true flavor of the tea. In truth, much less is required in this way than under the old and common practice.

The "old and common practice" that Mrs. Alcott referred to was putting the tea leaves in the teapot first and then pouring boiling water over them to fill the teapot. She preferred putting the tea leaves in *after* she had filled the teapot with boiling water.

Here is a more precise recipe for making the tea:

Bring a quart of fresh cold water to a boil. Meanwhile, heat the teapot by filling it with hot water. Just before the kettle comes to a boil, pour the water out of the teapot. Pour the boiling water into the teapot and spoon in about two tablespoons of loose tea leaves. Stir the leaves into the water with a spoon and let the tea steep (or "draw") for a few minutes.

Pour the tea through a strainer into teacups. Add hot water to the tea if it is too strong. Serve the tea with milk or sliced lemon and sugar.

Jo's Campfire Coffee

So Jo, feeling that her late lessons in cookery were to do her honor, went to preside over the coffee-pot, while the children collected dry sticks, and the boys made a fire, and got water from a spring near by.

—Little Women, *Chapter Twelve*

Coffee was considered a special-occasion treat. Jo and Meg drank coffee at the Gardiners' New Year's Eve party and Hannah had a pot ready to serve to the girls after Marmee left for Washington to care for Mr. March in the hospital. Later, Jo, having learned the hard way that she should master the basics of cookery before attempting fancy dinner parties, exhibited her expertise with coffee by making a pot for lunch at "Camp Laurence," Laurie's croquet party at Longmeadow.

There are many methods for making coffee. Today we have all sorts of electric appliances that brew it easily and automatically. In Jo's day, however, the appliances consisted of an open fire (or a fire in the cookstove) and a large metal coffeepot. At that time, this was the most common method of making coffee:

1 egg white
1 cup cold water, divided
1 cup of ground, roasted coffee beans
2 quarts freshly boiling water

With a fork, whip the egg white with $^1/_2$ cup cold water; add the ground coffee beans and stir until it is thoroughly moistened.

Scald the coffeepot with a little boiling water, add the coffee and egg mixture, and pour in the rest of the boiling water. Stop up the spout (with a cork or twisted bit of clean toweling) and set the pot on a grate in the fire or on the stove. Boil the coffee for five minutes. Remove the pot from the fire and immediately pour in the remaining cold water; be careful of the steam when you open the lid of the coffeepot. Let the coffee stand for three minutes so the grounds settle. Pour the coffee through a strainer into another heated pot or individual cups.

Serve the coffee with cream and sugar.

This makes about sixteen cups of coffee, plenty for the "Camp Laurence" crowd. You may want to reduce the quantity if you are serving a smaller group. Use one tablespoon of ground coffee for each eight ounces of water, no matter which method of brewing you choose, this one or a more modern one.

Amy's Refreshing Lemonade

. . . Beth took off her dusty boots and Amy made lemonade for the refreshment of the whole party. —Little Women, *Chapter Eleven*

The March girls were celebrating the beginning of the summer months. Both Meg and Jo were free from their jobs—Meg as governess to the King children and Jo as Aunt March's companion—and Beth and Amy were ready for a break from their lessons. They envisioned three months of sleeping late, reading stacks of books, learning new songs, and drawing lots of pictures. While they daydreamed of "fun forever, and no grubbing!," they sipped the lemonade Amy had made for them.

For two quarts of lemonade, you will need:

1   cup sugar
3   lemons
1   cup boiling water
6   cups cold water
Ice cubes
Thin lemon slices and/or fresh
        mint

Dissolve the sugar in the boiling water. Cut the lemons in half and squeeze out the juice. Strain the juice into a pitcher. Add the sugar water and mix well. Add the six cups of cold water and stir.

Serve the lemonade over ice in tall glasses. Garnish with thin slices of lemon and/or sprigs of fresh mint if desired.

Amy would have chipped off a few chunks of the large block of ice in the refrigerator to serve with her lemonade. The ice would have been purchased in town or from a delivery wagon. In winter, large chunks of ice were cut when the river was frozen and stored in special ice-houses with very thick walls. Sawdust was packed around the ice to insulate it further. The ice would last well into the summer using this method and was sold to the townspeople as they needed it.

The March family had a refrigerator but it was not an electric one, such as we have today, and it could not freeze ice. It would have been made of wood, like a small cabinet, and would have been lined with metal. It would have had one or two small storage compartments. The Marches would buy a large block of ice and set it in the special compartment or "ice-box" at the top of the small insulated refrigerator. It would keep the contents cold for a day or two.

Beth's Biscuits

Beth clapped her hands, regardless of the biscuit she held, and Jo tossed up her napkin, crying, "A letter! a letter! Three cheers for father!" —Little Women, *Chapter One*

Biscuits are traditionally served with afternoon tea and, in the Marches' case, with supper. They are quick and easy to make, and are best served hot with butter and jam.

> 1$^1/_2$ cups sifted flour
> 1 tablespoon baking powder
> $^1/_2$ teaspoon baking soda
> $^1/_2$ teaspoon salt
> 3 tablespoons lard or vegetable shortening
> $^3/_4$ cup buttermilk

Preheat the oven to 450 degrees.

Mix flour, baking powder, soda, and salt in a large mixing bowl. Cut in shortening with a fork or pastry cutter until mixture is blended. Stir in buttermilk and blend quickly with a fork until a soft dough is formed.

On a floured board, knead the dough lightly until it is smooth. Pat the dough out to a thickness of about $^1/_2$ inch. Cut into 1$^1/_2$-inch rounds with a biscuit cutter. Place rounds on an ungreased baking sheet and bake at 450 degrees for twelve minutes or until lightly browned.

Serve hot with butter and jam.

Jo's Bread-and-Butter Sandwiches

"Hurry and get done! Don't stop to quirk your little finger, and simper over your plate, Amy," cried Jo, choking in her tea, and dropping her bread, butter side down, on the carpet, in her haste to get at the treat.

—Little Women, *Chapter One*

The "treat" Jo was in such a hurry "to get at" was a letter from Father who was serving as an Army chaplain many miles away. The treats Jo and Amy were in the midst of eating were open-faced bread-and-butter sandwiches made from Hannah's delicious homemade bread, but you can use any kind of bread you like for yours.

> Thinly sliced bread
> Softened butter

Spread a slice of bread with a thin layer of butter. (Place another slice on top if you wish.) Trim off the crusts of the bread and slice the sandwich into four triangles or three "fingers."

Place sandwiches on a pretty plate (or line a plain plate with a lacy paper doily). Cover with a damp tea towel until you are ready to serve.

Allow three or four small sandwiches per guest.

If you wish, you may add a layer of watercress, thinly sliced cucumber, or jam on the buttered bread or mix one of the following into the softened butter before spreading it on the bread:

> Chopped fresh herbs such as
>   parsley, chives, or lemon balm
> Grated lemon or orange rind and
>   powdered sugar
> Cinnamon and brown sugar
> Honey or maple syrup

Christmas Morning Muffins

"I shall take the cream and the muffins," added Amy, heroically giving up the articles she most liked.

—Little Women, *Chapter Two*

Marmee had persuaded her daughters to take their fine Christmas breakfast of muffins, buckwheat cakes, and other special treats to the poor Hummel family whose six children, mother, and newborn baby were cold and hungry.

You can make these muffins for any breakfast or for teatime; perhaps you would like to make some to share.

1 egg
$^1/_2$ cup milk
$^1/_4$ cup oil
$1^1/_2$ cups flour
$^1/_2$ cup sugar
2 teaspoons baking powder
$^1/_4$ teaspoon salt
1 cup raisins (or other dried fruit, such as cranberries or chopped apricots)

Preheat the oven to 400 degrees.

Mix the egg, milk, and oil; add the flour, sugar, baking powder, and salt. Blend well but do not overmix. Stir in the fruit.

Fill greased or paper-lined muffin cups two-thirds full. Bake in a 400-degree oven 20–25 minutes.

Makes twelve muffins.

A "LITTLE FEAST" FOR CHRISTMAS EVENING

There was ice cream—actually two dishes of it, pink and white—and cake and fruit and distracting French bon-bons, and, in the middle of the table, four great bouquets of hot-house flowers!

—Little Women, *Chapter Two*

Just imagine the wide eyes of the March girls and their friends when they came downstairs from the premiere performance of *Operatic Tragedy* to see the elegant little feast that old Mr. Laurence had sent over. He had heard that the girls had given their Christmas breakfast that morning to the Hummel family and so sent over "a few trifles in honor of the day."

Perhaps you would like to prepare a similar "little feast" of your own "to express your friendly feeling" for your friends at Christmas or for any other special occasion.

White Christmas Cake

This is a fine cake to serve with the fruit compote that follows.

$^2/_3$ cup butter
$1^1/_2$ cups sugar
1   teaspoon vanilla extract
$^1/_2$ teaspoon almond extract
$2^1/_2$ cups white cake flour
$2^1/_2$ teaspoons baking powder
$^2/_3$ cup milk
4   egg whites
$^1/_2$ teaspoon salt
$^1/_2$ teaspoon cream of tartar
White Buttercream Icing
      (recipe follows)
Vanilla ice cream (optional)
Strawberry ice cream
      (optional)

Preheat the oven to 375 degrees. Grease and flour two 9-inch cake pans.

Cream butter until light. Add the sugar and beat until fluffy. Add vanilla and almond extracts. Sift together flour and baking powder and add to the creamed mixture alternately with the milk, beating until smooth.

In a separate bowl with clean beaters, beat egg whites until foamy. Add the salt and cream of tartar. Fold the egg whites and flour mixture together.

Pour the batter into the two cake pans. Bake at 375 degrees on a rack in the center of the oven for 20–25 minutes. Cool the layers for ten minutes on a wire rack; turn layers out onto racks to cool completely.

Frost with White Buttercream Icing:

6   tablespoons softened butter
4   cups confectioners' sugar,
      sifted
$^1/_2$ teaspoon salt
1   tablespoon vanilla

Cream the butter and the sugar. Add the salt and vanilla. If the icing is too thick, add a few drops of milk; if it is too thin, add a little more sugar.

Frost the cake layers and decorate as you wish, perhaps with sprigs of holly or sprinkle crushed peppermint candy canes around the outer edge of the cake.

Serve with a small scoop of vanilla ice cream and a small scoop of strawberry ice cream, if you wish.

Christmas Fruit Compote

Any kind of fruit in the wintertime in New England was considered a great delicacy because it had to be brought in from tropical climates by ship or train, expensive methods during Louisa May Alcott's era.

To make your own fruit compote, slice oranges, bananas, apples, or other seasonal fruits into a serving bowl. Add grapes if desired. Pour just enough orange juice over the fruit to moisten it. In order to serve six, you will need about four cups of chopped fruit. Garnish with chopped nuts, fresh or toasted shredded coconut, or sweetened whipped cream.

Distracting French Bonbons

Bonbons are creamy bite-size candies that are sometimes dipped in a chocolate glaze.

Mr. Laurence would have given the Marches *real* French bonbons, imported from France by ship. But here is an easy version you can make on your own.

3	tablespoons butter
4	tablespoons cream cheese
1¾	cups confectioners' sugar, sifted
½	teaspoon vanilla or other flavoring

Optional:

Granulated sugar *or*
½ pound chocolate morsels

Let butter and cream cheese soften. Cream the butter and cream cheese. Slowly add the sugar, beating until the mixture is light. Mix in vanilla. Color the mixture with a drop of food coloring, if you wish, for a delicate pastel look. Chill the mixture about an hour or until it is firm enough to work with.

With scrupulously clean hands, pinch off pieces of the mixture and roll them into bite-size balls (no more than one inch in diameter). If you do not plan to coat the bonbons with chocolate, roll them in granulated sugar for extra sparkle.

Set the bonbon pieces in a single layer on a cookie sheet lined with foil or parchment paper until they are firm, about one to two hours.

If you decide to coat the bonbons in chocolate, wait until after they are firm. Then, melt the chocolate morsels according to package directions (over hot water or even in the microwave). Using a toothpick or bamboo skewer, dip each bonbon piece in the chocolate until it is covered completely. (You may need to reheat the chocolate from time to time to keep it soft enough to dip.) Set the bonbon on a piece of waxed paper, remove the toothpick, and let the chocolate cool and harden.

When the chocolate is completely set, serve the bonbons on your prettiest serving plate. To store the bonbons, place them in a single layer in an airtight container and refrigerate.

Hannah's "Muffs"

These turn-overs were an institution; and the girls called them "muffs," for they had no others, and found the hot pies very comforting to their hands on cold mornings.

—Little Women, *Chapter Four*

A "muff" was a popular winter accessory carried by ladies in the *Little Women* era; it was usually made of fur. Both hands could be slipped inside the muff to keep warm. Since the Marches were too poor to afford fur muffs, they carried hot turnovers in their pockets to keep their hands warm. Later, they could eat the turnovers for lunch!

Hannah probably filled the "muffs" with apples since they were plentiful, inexpensive, and kept well over winter. Although it was common to fry the apple turnovers, Hannah probably baked these so that grease would not stain the girls' clothes.

To make "muffs," you will need:

Piecrust for two pies:

2	cups flour
$1\frac{1}{2}$	teaspoons sugar
$\frac{1}{2}$	teaspoon salt
1	cup shortening

$^1/_4$ cup water
$1^1/_2$ teaspoons white vinegar
1 egg, beaten

Filling:

3 medium-sized apples
3 tablespoons sugar
$^3/_4$ teaspoon cinnamon
2 teaspoons flour

PIECRUST: Mix flour, sugar, and salt for the piecrust with a fork in a large bowl. Add shortening and mix with the fork or a pastry cutter until mixture is crumbly.

In a small bowl, mix together the water, vinegar, and half of the beaten egg, about 2 tablespoons. (Save the rest of the egg for glazing the tops of the "muffs" or pies.) Pour this into the flour mixture and stir until all ingredients are moistened.

Chill the dough while you prepare the filling and preheat the oven to 425 degrees.

FILLING: Peel the apples and cut them into $^1/_4$-inch slices, removing the core. In a medium bowl, toss the apple slices with the sugar, cinnamon, and flour.

Roll out the piecrust on a floured board and cut it into four 6-inch circles, using a saucer as a guide.

Spoon about 3 tablespoons of the apple mixture onto each piecrust circle. Moisten the rim of each circle with a few drops of water. Fold each circle in half over the filling. Press the piecrust edges together firmly, then press the tip of a fork all around the edge to hold it together. Prick the top of the "muff" several times with the fork.

Place the "muffs" on a baking sheet. Brush beaten egg over the tops. Bake the "muffs" at 425 degrees for about 25 minutes or until golden brown.

Serve warm or at room temperature. Sprinkle with powdered sugar if desired.

Makes 4 "muffs."
Be sure to wrap each "muff" in a napkin before putting it in your pocket!

Jo's Cards of Gingerbread

Jo remembered the kind old gentleman, who used to let her build railroads and bridges with his big dictionaries, tell her stories about the queer pictures in his Latin books, and buy her cards of gingerbread whenever he met her in the street.

—Little Women, *Chapter Four*

One reason Jo didn't mind too much being Aunt March's companion was the opportunity to use Uncle March's vast library at Plumfield. We don't know much about Uncle March, just that he was wealthy, kind, and had died some years before.

The "cards of gingerbread" that Uncle March had bought for Jo were gingerbread cookies, like our gingerbread men of today, and were sold by bake

shops and street vendors in the late 1800s.

To make "cards of gingerbread," you will need:

2 tablespoons butter, softened
$\frac{1}{4}$ cup white or brown sugar
$\frac{1}{4}$ cup molasses
$1\frac{3}{4}$ cups flour
$\frac{1}{2}$ teaspoon baking soda
$\frac{1}{8}$ teaspoon ground cloves
$\frac{1}{4}$ teaspoon ground cinnamon
$\frac{1}{2}$ teaspoon ground ginger
$\frac{1}{4}$ teaspoon salt
2 tablespoons water

Preheat the oven to 350 degrees.

Beat the butter and sugar together until creamy. Stir in the molasses. Mix the flour, baking soda, cloves, cinnamon, ginger, and salt and add to the butter mixture alternately with the water, one third of each at a time. The dough will be stiff.

On a lightly floured board, roll the dough into a rectangle about $\frac{1}{4}$ inch thick. Using a ruler as a guide, trim the edges of the dough with a sharp knife or pastry wheel. Cut the dough into rectangles about 3" × 4". With a wide spatula, transfer the "cards" to a lightly greased baking sheet. Bake for about 8 minutes. Cool the "cards" on a wire rack. When completely cool, decorate in pretty designs with white Royal Icing:

76

1   egg white
$1^3/_4$ cup confectioners' sugar
2   tablespoons lemon juice

Beat egg white until stiff (but not dry). Gradually add the sugar and the lemon juice. Mix until thick. Cover the bowl with a damp towel.

To decorate gingerbread cards, spoon a few tablespoons of icing into a sandwich-size plastic bag. Snip off a bottom corner of the bag to make a tiny hole. Press the icing through the hole to make lacy designs on the gingerbread. Replenish the icing in the bag as necessary. Set the cookies aside in a single layer so that the icing can dry.

Meg's Blancmange

Jo ... showed the blanc-mange, surrounded by a garland of green leaves, and the scarlet flowers of Amy's pet geranium.
—Little Women, *Chapter Five*

Blancmange, a type of vanilla custard, was Meg's specialty. It was considered an elegant dessert in the Victorian era and was also a favorite dish to serve those who were recovering from an illness be-cause it is light and easily digestible. Jo took a dish of it to Laurie when she first visited him at his grandfather's house next door; Laurie had been sick with a cold. He thought the dessert almost "too pretty to eat."

Blancmange, along with strawberries and cream, was also to be the dessert at the "feast" Jo decided to prepare by herself for her sisters, Laurie, and the curious and talkative Miss Crocker. Unfortunately, nothing Jo put on the table that day was very appetizing—the blancmange was lumpy, the cream had soured, and Jo had "sugared" the strawberries with salt!

To make blancmange, you will need:

5   tablespoons cornstarch
4   cups milk
$^1/_2$ cup sugar
Pinch salt
2   eggs, separated
1   teaspoon vanilla

Mix the cornstarch with a little of the milk and blend it well, until it is smooth. Pour it and the rest of the milk into the top of a double boiler and add the sugar, salt, and beaten egg yolks. Heat water in the bottom of the double boiler to boiling; cook the mixture over simmering water 12 minutes, stirring it constantly.

Beat the egg whites until soft peaks form. Stir half the egg whites into the blancmange mixture; stir in the remaining egg whites and mix lightly.

Take the mixture off the heat and the hot water and let it cool. It will thicken as it cools. Add the vanilla.

Pour the mixture into a lightly greased, four-cup mold (or individual molds) and chill until it is firm. Unmold the blancmange onto a pretty platter and decorate it with leaves and flowers, if you wish. Perhaps you have a "pet geranium" with scarlet flowers wintering in a sunny window, as Amy did!

Amy's Pickled Limes

During the next few minutes the rumor that Amy March had got twenty-four delicious limes (she ate one on the way), and was going to treat, circulated through her "set" and the attentions of her friends became quite overwhelming.

—Little Women, *Chapter Seven*

One of the most memorable scenes in *Little Women* is Mr. Davis's discovery that Amy had brought the forbidden pickled limes into his classroom. He forced her to throw them, two at a time, out the window. Then he struck her palm with a ruler and made her stand in front of the class until recess. After this series of humiliations, Amy never returned to school but studied at home with Beth.

Although Amy bought her limes for a penny apiece in town, they are not hard to make at home. They do take time to "cure," however, so you must be patient and wait about two weeks from the time you start them until you eat them.

We suggest you pickle just a few limes on your first try to see if you like them well enough to make an entire batch of twenty-five, enough for Amy's class! The recipe can be multiplied to make as many as you wish.

4   small limes

$^1/_2$ cups kosher (coarse, non-iodized) salt

A glass pan large enough to hold the limes upright in a single layer

$1^1/_2$ cups apple-cider vinegar

$1^1/_2$ cups white vinegar

$^1/_3$ cup sugar

$^1/_2$ ounce sliced ginger root

6   whole cloves

1   tablespoon black peppercorns

1   tablespoon mustard seeds

2   garlic cloves, peeled

Wash and dry the limes. Cut four slits lengthwise down the rind of each lime; do not cut quite through to the pulp. Pack the slits with salt (gently squeeze the lime to open the slits a bit so that you can get the salt in them). Set the limes on end in the dish, packed closely together. Cover the dish loosely with waxed paper. Turn the limes three or four times a day on their other ends, for three or four days. Repack slits with salt as necessary.

Remove the limes to a large heat-proof bowl or jar. Pour any juice left in the pan a large pot. Add the vinegars, sugar, and spices and bring it to a boil. Pour the brine over the limes. After the limes and vinegar cool, cover them and place them in the refrigerator. The limes should "cure" in their brine for at least

several days and as long as a week before serving.

The pickled limes can be eaten as a snack—cut the tops off and suck the juice out, as Amy and her friends did, or peel and slice them. They are quite tart, so you might want to dip them in sugar as you eat them. The limes can also be diced and used as a relish with meats or vegetables.

Jo's Strawberries and Cream

. . . the pretty glass plates went round, and every one looked graciously at the little rosy islands floating in a sea of cream.

—Little Women, *Chapter Eleven*

Strawberries and cream should have been a foolproof dessert for Jo's first dinner party. If only she had bought sweeter, riper berries; if only she had not been in such a hurry and made sure that she was sprinkling sugar instead of salt on them; if only she had remembered to keep the cream cold instead of letting it sit out in the hot kitchen!

To serve strawberries and cream as Jo intended to serve hers, you can pour the cream over the berries in dessert dishes or, for an extra-special treat, make whipped cream and top the berries with a spoonful or two. Whipping cream is easy for us today since we have electric mixers or mechanical beaters but in Jo's day, people had to use a wire whisk to beat the cream by hand. It took much longer and made their arms very tired!

For six servings:

1   quart fresh strawberries (ripe ones, of course!)

Sugar to taste, about $\frac{1}{3}$ cup (*not* salt!)

1   pint heavy cream (fresh and cold)

$\frac{1}{4}$ cup powdered sugar

$\frac{1}{2}$ teaspoon vanilla

Set aside six whole, perfect strawberries for garnish. Clean and hull the remaining berries. Slice the berries and place in a medium bowl. Sprinkle the sugar over them; stir them gently. Let them stand for 10 or 15 minutes while the sugar dissolves.

In a cold bowl, whip the cream with chilled beaters until it makes soft peaks. Stir in powdered sugar and vanilla. Chill the cream until you are ready to serve it.

Spoon the berries onto dessert plates and top with whipped cream. Garnish with the reserved berries.

Hannah's Just-in-Case Pies

Hannah "knocked up a couple of pies in case of company unexpected."

—Little Women, *Chapter Eighteen*

Beth was gravely ill with scarlet fever and Laurie had just informed Jo that he had already sent for Marmee. She was now on her way back from Washington where she had been caring for Mr. March. Hannah immediately headed for the kitchen to have some fresh pies ready for her arrival.

These "sugar pies" would have been quick to make and the ingredients would likely have been on hand in Hannah's kitchen for this late-night "emergency" baking. This recipe contains enough ingredients for two pies; use half the ingredients if you wish to make only one pie.

Piecrust for two pies (see page 75)

$\frac{1}{2}$ cup flour

2   cups sugar

Pinch salt

$\frac{1}{2}$ cup cold butter, cut in small pieces

2   cups heavy whipping cream

2   cups milk

2   teaspoons vanilla extract

Grated nutmeg

Preheat the oven to 350 degrees.

Roll out the chilled piecrust dough on a lightly floured board. Cut and fit the piecrust into two 9-inch pie pans; crimp the edges and chill.

Mix flour, sugar, and salt in a large bowl. With a pastry blender or a fork, cut the butter into the flour mixture until it is well blended. Add the cream and mix gently. Pour the mixture into the pie shells. Mix the milk and vanilla in a measuring cup and slowly pour them over the top of the cream mixture in the pie shells; do not stir. Sprinkle nutmeg over the tops of the pies.

Bake pies for $1^1/_2$ hours at 350 degrees. Remove pies from the oven (center will be soft) and cool them thoroughly on racks.

Makes two 9-inch pies.

Meg's Wedding Spice Cake

There was no display of gifts, for they were already in the little house, nor was there an elaborate breakfast, but a plentiful lunch of cake and fruit, dressed with flowers.

—Little Women, *Chapter Twenty-five*

A spicy fruitcake was considered the most elegant of wedding cakes in the *Little Women* era. Although the Marches did not bake Meg's cake (Laurie saw the cake being delivered to the house), it was "a remarkably plummy one" ("plummy" meaning full of raisins), perhaps similar to this one.

For a three-tiered cake, purchase a set of round wedding-cake pans or make a rectangular cake from one 13" × 9" pan, one 11" × 7" pan, and one 9" × 5" pan.

4	eggs
4	cups applesauce
2	cups vegetable oil
$2^1/_2$	cups brown sugar
2	teaspoons baking soda
4	teaspoons baking powder
1	teaspoon salt
4	teaspoons ground cinnamon
1	teaspoon ground cloves
1	teaspoon ground nutmeg
5	cups all-purpose flour
2	cups chopped walnuts
2	cups raisins

Preheat the oven to 350 degrees. Grease and flour the bottoms of the cake pans.

Beat eggs until frothy; add applesauce and oil and mix thoroughly. Stir in sugar, baking soda, baking powder, salt, and spices. Gradually add the flour and blend well. Stir in nuts and raisins.

Fill each pan to an equal depth

(about $1^3/_4$ inches deep). Bake the large layer 40 minutes or until it tests done (the cake will spring back when touched with a finger). Smaller layers should take less time to bake, about 25–30 minutes.

Remove layers from oven and cool in the pans on wire racks for 10 minutes. Turn the layers out of their pans onto wire racks to finish cooling. When they have cooled completely, frost with about 6 cups of your favorite white icing or this Cream Cheese Frosting:

3	8-ounce packages cream cheese
6	cups confectioners' sugar, sifted
$^3/_4$	cup cream or milk
2	tablespoons vanilla

Beat the cream cheese until soft and fluffy. Gradually beat in the sugar. Add the milk and vanilla and mix well.

To decorate the cake, brush any loose crumbs from the edges and bottoms of the cake layers. Place the large layer top down on a serving tray that is a little larger than the cake. Place 2-inch-wide strips of waxed paper under the edges of the cake to keep the icing off the tray.

Spread a thin layer of icing on the top and sides of the large layer to seal the surfaces. Spread a cupful of icing over the top and sides of the cake to cover it generously. Center the medium-size layer on top of the bottom layer and frost it as you did the first layer; repeat for the top layer.

Decorate the cake with fruits and flowers of your choice, such as pink roses and strawberries.

Keep the cake in a cool place until it is time to serve it.

Note: Cream cheese was not available commercially in the nineteenth century; each household made its own cream cheese from clabbered (sour) milk when they needed it for a recipe.

Meg's Newlywed Bread Pudding

The poor man was put through a course of bread pudding, hash, and warmed-over coffee, which tried his soul, although he bore it with praise-worthy fortitude.

—Little Women, *Chapter Twenty-eight*

Bread pudding is a thrifty but delicious old-fashioned dessert. When Meg and John were newlyweds, Meg enthusiastically cooked all sorts of fancy dishes. But when the household accounts were examined, "a frugal fit would ensue" and more economical fare had to be served. You will need the following ingredients to make Meg's bread pudding:

1	tablespoon softened butter
6	slices firm white bread with crusts removed
$^1/_4$	cup raisins
2	eggs
$^1/_3$	cup white sugar, divided
2	tablespoons brown sugar, divided
$^1/_2$	teaspoon vanilla extract
$^1/_4$	teaspoon ground cinnamon

Dash nutmeg (optional)
$1^1/_2$ cups milk
Hot water

Preheat the oven to 350 degrees. Lightly butter a one-quart baking dish.

Butter the bread slices on one side, cut them into one-inch cubes, and place them in the baking dish. Sprinkle the raisins over the top.

In a separate bowl, beat the eggs with half the white and brown sugar. Add the vanilla, spices, and milk. Mix well. Pour the mixture over the bread cubes and sprinkle the remaining sugar over the top.

Place the baking dish in a larger pan, such as a roasting pan, and set them in the oven. Pour hot water into the larger pan until it comes halfway up the sides of the baking dish.

Bake the pudding about 45 minutes. If a knife inserted into the center of the pudding comes out clean, the pudding is done. (You may need to bake it 5 or 10 more minutes.)

Remove the pudding from the oven and the pan of water and cool it in its baking dish on a wire rack. The pudding is delicious served warm or cold and can be served plain, or with heavy cream or ice cream—if the household accounts will allow it!

Laurie and Amy's Homecoming Tea-Tarts

Such a happy procession as filed away into the little dining room!

—Little Women, *Chapter Forty-three*

Laurie, Amy, and Mr. Laurence had just returned home from Europe and surprised everyone with the news that Laurie and Amy had been married six weeks before in Paris. There was a celebration for them that very evening at tea with gingerbread, hot biscuits, and "captivating little tarts" that Daisy and Demi, Meg and John's little three-year-old twins, seemed to think belonged in their pockets.

For 12 to 16 tarts, you will need:

Piecrust for two pies (see
    page 75)
Tart pan
3   eggs, beaten
$^2/_3$ cup sugar

$^1/_4$ teaspoon salt
$^1/_3$ cup melted butter
1   cup dark corn syrup
1   cup chopped walnuts

Preheat the oven to 375 degrees.

After making the piecrust dough, pinch off about a tablespoon of it, roll into a ball, and press the dough into each cup in the tart pan, forming the bottom and sides of the tart shell. Chill the tart shells while you are making the filling.

Mix together all the ingredients, stirring in the walnuts. Spoon the filling into the tart shells to within $^1/_4$ inch of the top of the shells.

Bake the tarts about 20 minutes; cool them before serving.

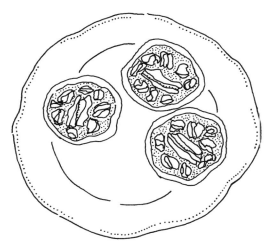

Professor Bhaer's Chocolate Drops

Demi . . . hadn't the heart to insult a rival who kept a mine of chocolate-drops in his waistcoat-pocket, and a watch that could be taken out of its case and freely shaken by ardent admirers.

—Little Women, *Chapter Forty-five*

Professor Bhaer loved children and they loved him. He always carried little candies for them in his pockets, had interesting stories to tell and new games to play. Chocolate drops were a favorite of Demi's and kept him happy even when he became aware that Jo seemed to be paying more attention to the professor than she was to him!

Professor Bhaer would have purchased his chocolate drops from a candy maker in town, but you can make this simple version in your own kitchen.

1   12-ounce bag semi-sweet chocolate morsels
1   ounce tiny white or colored nonpareils or candy sprinkles (optional)

In a bowl set in a pan of hot water, stir the chocolate morsels until they are melted. (Add more hot water to the pan as necessary.)

Drop the melted chocolate by half-teaspoonfuls onto waxed paper spread on a cookie sheet. While the chocolate is still soft, sprinkle the top of each chocolate drop with the nonpareils, if desired. Let the chocolate harden in a cool place.

When the chocolate drops are firm, lift them from the waxed paper with a spatula. Place them in a pretty candy box or make a paper cone like the ones that were popular in Victorian times. To make

your cone, start by cutting a 10-inch circle from a piece of pretty gift-wrap paper. Place the circle face down on a table. Fold the circle in half, then fold the half-circle into thirds, as shown, until a cone shape is formed. Secure the open side with a bit of tape or a decorative sticker. Cut a scalloped edge at the top if you wish. Gently open the cone. Attach a 12-inch piece of ribbon for a "handle" if you wish. Fill the cone with chocolate drops.

To serve the candy-filled cone, set it

in a glass goblet or vase to hold it upright. To give the cone as a gift, wrap a sheet of clear cellophane or plastic wrap around it, tying the wrap at the top of the cone with a ribbon.

Daisy's Patty-Cake Cookies

I put it to any lady if it was not hard to have one dozen delicious patties (made of flour, salt, and water, with a large raisin in the middle of each, and much sugar over the whole) swept away at one fell swoop?
—Little Men, *Chapter Nine*

Daisy, Nan, and Bess had cooked up some treats on Daisy's little cookstove and three of the Plumfield boys were invited to share them at a "ball." Every-

one dressed up in such finery as they could put together, tried to mind their manners, and danced the polka. Finally, it was time for "tea"—bread and butter, pie, soft custards, and "a large plate of patties." The patties, unfortunately, ended up as "very effective missiles, being nearly as hard as bullets" in the hands of the arguing boys.

To make delicious "patties" that are more likely to be eaten than used as missiles, you will need more than just the flour, salt, and water Daisy used:

$^3/_4$ cup softened butter
1   egg
$^1/_2$ teaspoon vanilla
1   cup sugar, divided
2   cups all-purpose flour
$^1/_4$ teaspoon baking powder
Pinch salt
$^1/_2$ cup seedless raisins

Combine the butter, egg, vanilla, and $^1/_2$ cup sugar in a mixing bowl and beat them until fluffy. Add the flour, baking powder, and salt and mix well. Chill the dough for about two hours.

Preheat the oven to 350 degrees.

Place $^1/_2$ cup sugar in a small bowl or saucer. Pinch off bits of dough and roll between your palms to make 1-inch balls. Roll each ball in sugar and place on an ungreased cookie sheet about 2 inches apart. Pat each ball to flatten slightly. Press one raisin in the center of each cookie.

Bake 10–12 minutes at 350 degrees. Remove cookies to a wire rack and cool.

Marmee's "Personality" Cookies

. . . Mr. Laurie cried out, "Bless my heart, I forgot grandma's bundle!" and running out to the carriage, returned with an interesting white parcel, which, being opened, disclosed a choice collection of beasts, birds, and pretty things cut out of crisp sugary cake and baked a lovely brown.

—Little Men, *Chapter Eleven*

Marmee had baked sugar cookies for the Plumfield children and had cut each in a different shape for each child—"a fish for Dan, a fiddle for Nat, a book for Demi," and so on.

Why not bake a batch of "personality" cookies for your own friends and family? Think about what each person likes and cut out that shape in the cookie dough, either with a cookie cutter or with a sharp knife and a pattern. (If you prefer, you can bake the cookies in squares or rounds and decorate them in special designs with icing.)

You can use this recipe for "crisp sugary cakes," adapted from Mrs. Alcott's own recipe for "tea cakes," or your own favorite sugar cookie recipe.

1	pound flour (4 cups)
1	pound sugar (2 cups)
1	teaspoon saleratus (baking soda)
1	egg
1	cup milk
3	ounces softened butter (6 tablespoons)

Being an experienced cook, Mrs. Alcott did not need to write down the directions for mixing the dough. She would have first mixed the flour, sugar, and saleratus in a large bowl and added the egg, milk, and softened butter to them and mixed them well with a wooden spoon. Then she would have been ready to roll the dough to a half-inch thickness, which would be for "tea cakes."

In order to make cookies with definite shapes, chill the dough and roll it about $1/4$ inch thick on a floured board. Choose a different cookie cutter for each person you want to give a cookie to. Make sure the shape represents something unique about each person (preferably something complimentary!). Press the cookie cutters into the rolled-out cookie dough and place the cut-out shapes on a cookie sheet. If you don't have a cookie cutter in the shape you want, draw a shape on lightweight cardboard, cut it out, place it on the cookie dough, and cut around it with a small sharp knife.

Bake at 350 degrees for 8 minutes. After allowing the cookies to cool on a wire rack, decorate each cookie as you wish—with colored icing, sugar sprinkles, or other decorations.

Marmee's Cookie Parcel

To present your cookies in a "white parcel," as Marmee did, select a shallow white box and decorate the lid with the cookie shapes you used for the real cookies. Just trace around the clean cookie cutters with different-colored pens directly on the box lid. Line the box with waxed paper or doilies and place the cookies carefully in the box. Protect the cookies with a sheet of waxed paper between each layer.

Asia's Gingersnaps

"I actually smelt the coffee we used to have, and one night I nearly cried when I woke from a dream of Asia's ginger cookies."

—Jo's Boys, *Chapter Eighteen*

Emil, Professor Bhaer's nephew, had just returned from his sailing adventures—with his bride, Mary. He told of being shipwrecked and so hungry that he actually dreamed of the coffee and cookies he used to love at Plumfield. Asia, Plumfield's cook, always kept a supply of gingersnaps on hand to feed the population of hungry boys and girls that swarmed over the Bhaers' campus. She stored them in a tin box so they would stay fresh.

Here is a recipe for gingersnaps that was a favorite in the Alcotts' home, found in Mrs. Alcott's recipe book of 1856:

Half pound butter, half sugar, two and one half flour, 1 pint molasses, teaspoon soda, carraway seed or ginger. Roll very thin and bake a few minutes.

In today's recipe terms, it would read this way:

$1/_2$ pound (2 sticks) softened butter or margarine
1   cup sugar
2   cups molasses
3   cups flour
1   teaspoon baking soda
1   teaspoon ground ginger (or caraway seeds)

Preheat the oven to 350 degrees.

Cream the butter and sugar until they are fluffy. Add the molasses and mix well. Stir the flour, baking soda, and ginger together and add them to the molasses mixture. Mix until a stiff dough forms.

Roll the dough out on a flour-dusted board with a flour-dusted rolling pin to about $1/_8$-inch thickness. Cut in rounds with a floured cutter or juice glass.

Bake on a lightly greased cookie sheet for about 8 minutes.

Remove the cookies from the cookie sheet and cool them on a wire rack.

Gingersnaps keep for a long time if they are stored in an airtight container, but you will have to hide the container because these cookies are so tasty, they will disappear quickly!

To make Gingerbread Nuts like those Jo took with her on the train to New York, make the recipe above but instead of rolling out the dough, pinch off bits of dough and roll them into nut-like balls. If you like, shape them to resemble walnuts, pecans, almonds, or even acorns. Roll them in sugar and bake them at 350 degrees for 8 minutes.

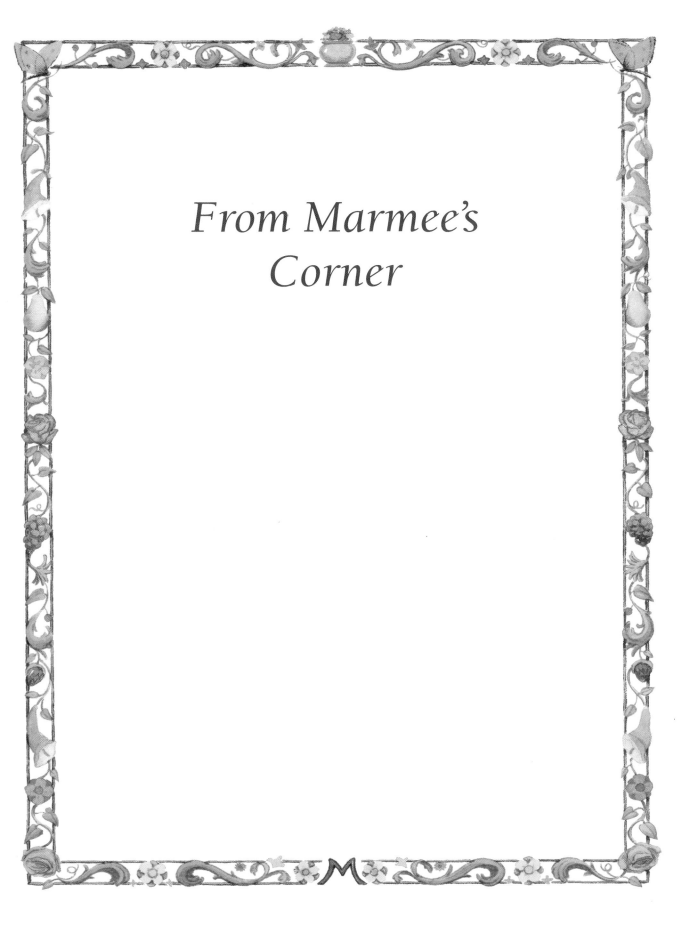

From Marmee's Corner

Activities from the
Little Women Series

"May we, Mother?" asked Meg, turning to Mrs. March, who sat sewing in what they called "Marmee's Corner."

—Little Women, *Chapter Eleven*

Each of the March girls knew how to sew and knit and each produced her share of the family's clothing and linens. They loved to sit together in the evening with Marmee to share the news of the day while they stitched up the long seams of skirts or sheets or mended their stockings.

In spare moments, however, usually in the afternoon, each had a different favorite activity with which to amuse herself. Meg loved designing the latest fashions and sewing fanciful creations. Jo wrote plays and stories. Beth made objects from things she collected outdoors. Amy sketched and painted. On special occasions, such as birthdays and Christmas, the Marches, like the Alcotts, made many of their gifts for each other. Other favorite activities were the plays and entertainments the March girls performed for which they created the costumes and props.

In this chapter there are directions for making some of the things the March girls enjoyed so that you can bring a bit of the world of *Little Women* into your own.

Putting Together Your Own "Little Work-Basket"

Then out came the four little work-baskets, and the needles flew. . . .

—Little Women, *Chapter One*

All of the March girls learned to sew when they were very young, just as most girls of the era did. There was always sewing to be done, for the women in the family made most of the family's clothes and household items, including sheets, pillowcases, quilts, and towels. Mending was another of their frequent activities.

Each girl had her own "work-basket" in which she kept her sewing tools as well as the projects she was work-ing on at the time. Here is how to make a "little work-basket" of your own, very useful when buttons need sewing on, hems need to be restitched, or a patch needs to be put on your skirt if you have stood too close to the fire!

You will need:

1 small-to-medium basket with a lid, if possible

Furnish your work basket with small sewing scissors, needles of assorted sizes, straight pins, a thimble, spools of threads in several colors, a cloth tape measure, a small covered jar or tin for buttons, and any other sewing notions you wish.

You will also need a pincushion. You can purchase one or you can make one like many of the women of the Marches' era used:

2 squares of felt, 3" × 3"
1 yard $\frac{1}{2}$-inch grosgrain ribbon
Stuffing
Needle and thread
Scissors

Put the two felt squares together and stitch them together on three sides $\frac{1}{4}$ inch from the edges. Stuff the pocket tightly and slip one end of the ribbon about 1 inch into the open end of the cushion. Stitch the opening closed as you did for the other sides. Put a few straight pins in the pincushion.

Tie the other end of the ribbon through one of the finger holes of your small sewing scissors. When you are sewing, wear the ribbon around your neck with the pincushion hanging down on one side and the scissors on the other so that your most important sewing tools will always be close at hand.

Birthday Crown

"I used to be so frightened when it was my turn to sit in the big chair with the crown on, and see you all come marching around to give the presents, with a kiss."

—Little Women, *Chapter One*

Celebrating birthdays in grand style was a March (and Alcott) family tradition—presents, music, marches, picnics, and games were usually part of the celebration and the birthday person always wore a special crown. Shy Beth liked the presents and their accompanying kisses but not being the center of attention. The other girls, of course, loved it!

Make a birthday crown for your next birthday party. Any leftover gold paper and trimmings can be made into "gold-paper jewelry" such as the March girls made for their theatrical productions.

You will need:

1 piece heavy gold paper,
    about 28" × 6"
Scissors
Gold paper gift-wrap ribbon
Glue
Small beads, sequins, colored
    ribbon, small buttons
    (optional)
Safety pin or paper clip

Cut points into one long edge of the gold paper as shown. Glue gold ribbon to the pointed edge and let it dry.

If you wish, glue on small beads, sequins, bits of colored ribbon, or small buttons for "jewels" around the crown.

Pin or paper clip the ends of the crown together to fit the head of the birthday person.

Beth's Marked Handkerchiefs

"How nice my handkerchiefs look, don't they? Hannah washed and ironed them for me, and I marked them all myself," said Beth, looking proudly at the somewhat uneven letters which had cost her such labor.

—Little Women, *Chapter Two*

"Marking" handkerchiefs and other linens meant embroidering one's initials or name on them, which was very popular in the Victorian era. Sometimes, instead of thread, an especially sentimental girl would use strands of her long hair to mark handkerchiefs for her sweetheart, as Daisy did for Nat in *Jo's Boys*. Handkerchiefs were usually marked (or monogrammed) in one corner; towels and pillowcases would be marked at the center of one side, near the hemline.

Marking requires an embroidery hoop for best results—it keeps the fabric taut, making it easier to sew the stitches evenly. Since it is difficult to place the corner of a handkerchief in an embroidery hoop, baste four handkerchiefs together into one large square and place them in the hoop so that the four corners are centered (see illustration); in this way four can be marked without removing the hoop. If you want to mark just one handkerchief, baste some scraps of material onto the two sides of the handkerchief corner so they can be stretched into

the hoop's rim and the area to be marked is in the center of the hoop.

For one handkerchief:

$8^1/_2$-inch-square fine white
    cotton fabric (or a ready-
    made white handkerchief)
Needle and white thread
Monogram transfers or tailor's
    chalk pencil
1 skein embroidery floss,
    white or pastel color
1 embroidery needle
Small sewing scissors
Small embroidery hoop

To hem the fabric, turn down $^1/_8$ inch (or less) all around and press flat with a hot iron; fold edges over again and press flat. Pin the folds and hand stitch with the tiniest stitches possible.

Press one monogram letter transfer on a corner of the handkerchief (according to the directions on the package) or sketch a letter with the tailor's chalk pencil. You may use more than one letter, or a name, if you prefer.

Place a corner of the handkerchief in the embroidery hoop, making sure it is stretched tightly. Use the procedure described above to baste scraps of fabric onto the edges of the handkerchief if necessary.

Thread the needle with one 24-inch strand of embroidery floss. To get started,

stitch a couple of tiny horizontal stitches to hold the thread in place without having to knot the end of it. Make several rows of vertical-running stitches within the outlines of the letter. Make a couple of horizontal stitches to hold the thread in place. Clip the end of the thread.

Using a double strand of floss, satin-stitch (horizontal stitches close together) the monogram, keeping the edges as even as possible. To get started, hold about an inch of the ends of the floss with your thumb against the running stitches you made. This loose end will be covered and held in place with the satin stitches, eliminating the need for a knot at the end of the thread.

To finish, run an inch or so of thread underneath the satin stitches of the monogram and clip the thread.

Press the handkerchief and fold it so that the monogram is visible.

Hand-marked handkerchiefs are rare these days; they make wonderful gifts, not only for mothers but for other family members and friends. A bride-to-be perhaps would find it useful for catching a few tears of joy as her friends gather 'round her to wish her well.

Marmee's Christmas Gift Basket

". . . have everything ready," said Meg, looking over the presents, which were collected in a basket and kept under the sofa, ready to be produced at the proper time.

—Little Women, *Chapter Two*

The March girls had decided to forgo presents for themselves in order to buy presents for their beloved "Marmee." They did not have a Christmas tree under which to place their presents—it was not yet customary for homes to have their own Christmas trees—so they placed their presents for Marmee in a basket and brought it out on Christmas morning after they had returned from taking their special breakfast feast to the Hummels.

None of the presents was wrapped in gift paper (Jo thought even tying ribbons on them was silly!) but each was accompanied by a note. Beth gave Amy "her finest rose" to put with the bottle of cologne Amy had bought for Marmee since she had, at the last minute, exchanged the small bottle she had originally bought for a larger one.

The March girls may have covered the basket of unwrapped gifts with a pretty cloth to hide the gifts inside until they were ready to give them to Marmee.

To make your own version of this gift basket, you will need:

- 1 large shallow basket with handles
- Length of fabric in Christmas colors, large enough to line and drape over the edges of the basket
- 2 yards of $^3/_4$-inch-wide satin or grosgrain ribbon in a color that coordinates with the fabric
- $1^1/_3$ yards of $^1/_4$-inch coordinating satin or grosgrain ribbon
- 4 small bells

Finish the edges of the fabric with a hem or pinking shears; place the fabric in the basket, right side up. Let the edges of the fabric hang over the rim of the basket.

Cut the $^3/_4$-inch ribbon in two; each piece should be 1 yard long. Thread one length through each handle and tie each into a large, pretty bow.

Cut the $^1/_4$-inch ribbon into two 24-inch lengths. As you did with the wider ribbon, thread one length of the $^1/_4$-inch ribbon through each handle and tie each in a small bow. Slip a small bell on each end of the $^1/_4$-inch ribbon and tie each end in a knot to hold the bells in place.

Fill the basket with gaily wrapped Christmas gifts for friends and family.

Jo's Theatrical Costume Box

Being still too young to go often to the theatre, and not rich enough to afford any great outlay for private performances, the girls put their wits to work and—necessity being the mother of invention—made whatever they needed.

—Little Women, *Chapter Two*

The March girls loved to put on plays for each other and, occasionally, for their friends, as they did that first Christmas—a dozen girls gathered at the March home to see the performance of *The Witch's Curse, an Operatic Tragedy.*

Jo, of course, wrote the plays and all the sisters acted them out, usually playing several different parts in each play. They made their own costumes, sets, and props, such as "paste-board guitars, antique lamps made of old-fashioned butter-boats covered with silver paper, gorgeous robes of old cotton, glittering with tin spangles from a pickle factory, and armor covered with the same useful diamond-shaped bits, left in sheets when the lids of tin preserve-pots were cut out." Jo always wrote parts for herself so that she could wear her most treasured costume—"russet-leather boots" and "slashed doublet"—and brandish an "old foil" (fencing sword).

The costumes were kept ready for instant use in a trunk in the garret. (The trunk that the Alcott girls used can still be seen at their home, Orchard House, with some of their costumes still in it, including the famous "russet-leather boots.")

Put together your own costume box so that you will be ready for the next "there's nothing to do" day.

In a large storage box, trunk, or old suitcase, place items that may come in

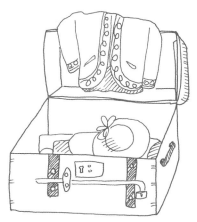

handy as set furnishings or costumes when you put on a play. Among the items you might include are: hats, scarves, shoes, lace collars, feather boas, costume jewelry, gloves that would otherwise be discarded. Be certain to have some cosmetics and face paints. Old sheets and bedspreads can be used for anything from capes to curtains. Don't forget to make some "gold paper jewelry" as the March girls did.

It would be fun to get together with your friends and write your own play, fashion the sets and costumes yourselves, and present the play to an audience of family members. During set changes and intermissions, "ushers" can serve refreshments, such as cookies and lemonade (see page 68), to the audience. It will be an "excellent drill for your memories, a harmless amusement, and will employ many hours which otherwise might be idle, lonely, or spent in less profitable society."

Beth's Ribbon Box

"And such lovely weather; I'm so glad of that," added Beth, tidily sorting neck and hair ribbons in her best box, lent for the great occasion.

—Little Women, *Chapter Nine*

Meg was about to leave for "Vanity Fair"—her two weeks of "novelty and pleasure" at the home of her friends, the Moffats. Her sisters and Marmee helped put together a trunkful of their best clothes and accessories for Meg to take with her—Jo contributed a new muslin skirt, Amy arranged pins "artistically" on Meg's pincushion, and Beth lent "her best box" for Meg to put her ribbons in.

Why not make a box *for* ribbons *with* ribbons? It will be very pretty on a bureau, in a drawer, or even in a "go-abroady" trunk, if you happen to have one.

You will need:

1 small-to-medium-sized
   box with a lid
Assorted ribbons, $1/2$ inch to
   1 inch wide
Scissors
Glue

Cut lengths of ribbon as wide as the box lid, plus an additional 1 inch; you will want to have enough to cover the entire width of the lid. Arrange the ribbons side by side on the lid so that they touch but don't overlap. Since the ribbon is 1 inch longer than the width of the box, there should be an extra $1/2$ inch on each end. Crease the $1/2$-inch ends and glue them down on the edges of the lid. Let the glue dry.

Cut more lengths of ribbon as long as the box lid; as before, each piece of ribbon should be 1 inch longer than the length of the box and you should cut enough to cover the entire lid. Begin

weaving these ribbons in and out of the ribbons already glued to the box lid.

Crease the $1/2$-inch ends and glue them on the edges of the lid. Trim any uneven ends. When the glue is dry, glue another ribbon all around the box lid to cover the ends of the woven strips. If you like, you can glue a decorative flower to the top of the box.

Arrange your hair ribbons and neck ribbons neatly in your ribbon box, as Beth did in hers.

Pickwick Club Badges

At seven o'clock the four members as-cended to the clubroom, tied their badges round their heads, and took their seats with great solemnity.

—Little Women, *Chapter Ten*

Besides their "theatricals," the March girls entertained themselves with weekly meet-ings of their "Pickwick Club," named for one of their favorite books by Charles Dickens, *The Posthumous Papers of the Pickwick Club*. For their meetings, each girl took the name of a character in the novel—Meg was Samuel Pickwick, Jo was Augustus Snodgrass, Beth was Tracy Tupman, and Amy was Nathaniel Winkle—and each wore a badge she had made with the name on one side, and the initials P.C. on the other. At the meetings, "Pickwick" read a copy of their newspa-per, *The Pickwick Portfolio*, that had been edited by "Snodgrass."

The "Pickwick Club" in *Little Women* was based on the Alcott sisters' own Pickwick Club, which they formed when they lived at Hillside in Concord. Their newspapers were entitled *The Olive Leaf* and *The Pickwick* and were hand-written by Louisa. Copies of these news-papers still exist, along with three of the Alcotts' own badges. Louisa's is the only one missing.

To make authentic Pickwick Club badges, you will need:

White lightweight cardboard
Scissors
Yarn
Colored pens or pencils

Cut strips of cardboard 10 inches long and $1\frac{3}{4}$ inches wide. Punch a small hole with the tip of a pencil, a needle, or a hole punch about $\frac{1}{2}$ inch from each end. Cut two pieces of yarn in lengths 5 inches shorter than the circumference of your head, and thread one piece through each hole. Tie a knot in the ends to keep the yarn from pulling through the holes.

Write the initials P.C. in large letters with colored pen or pencil in the center of one side of each badge. Turn the badges over and write the character name of a club member on each.

Place a badge around your head with your character's name across your forehead, then tie the yarn in a bow at the back of your head. When your "Pickwick Club" meeting is over, place the badges in a folder or a box so that they will be ready for the next meeting.

Laurie's Birdhouse "Post-Office"

"I merely wish to say, that as a slight token of my gratitude for the honor done me, and as a means of promoting friendly relations between adjoining nations, I have set up a post-office in the hedge in the lower corner of the garden . . ."

—Little Women, *Chapter Ten*

Laurie had transformed an old martin-house (a large birdhouse for a colony of purple martins to build nests in) into a private post office in which the Marches and Laurences could leave notes, invitations, and small gifts for each other. He "stopped up the door and made the roof open" to accommodate the volume and variety of mail that this flock of letter writers and gift givers were sure to gener-ate. Over the years, the post office held "tragedies and cravats, poetry and pick-les, garden-seeds and long letters, music and gingerbread, rubbers, invitations, scoldings and puppies" along with "odd bundles, mysterious messages, funny telegrams" and, of course, love letters!

To make a post office of your own, do as Laurie did and improvise—make one from something that is already on hand. If you don't happen to have an old "martin-house" in your garage, look for something else that would serve the pur-pose—a bird feeder, especially one with a cover that opens, would be a splendid post office, for instance. An upside-down flowerpot or a large covered pail might be just right for holding your messages; per-haps you will even find an old metal mailbox with a door and a signal flag to raise when there is a message inside.

If you want to make a simple bird-house to use as a post office, here is one that is easy to make. Be sure to ask an adult to help.

You will need:

Scraps of wood in these dimensions:
    3 square pieces—
        5" × 5" × $\frac{1}{4}$"
    4 rectangle pieces—
        5" × 6" × $\frac{1}{4}$"
Saw
Wood glue, or a wood-craft
    stapler and staples, or a
    hammer and small nails
1-inch brass hinge and
    screws, screwdriver
Exterior enamel or stain,
    moss and twigs, craft sticks,
    or other materials for
    decoration
Ribbon pieces in different
    colors, $\frac{1}{2}$" × 8" each—one
    piece for each message
    sender (optional)

Make two gabled end pieces from two of the rectangles: lay a 5-inch-square piece on top of a rectangle. Draw a line across the rectangle along the edge of the square piece as shown. At the top of the rectangle, make a dot at the center point. Draw a straight line from the center point down to the ends of the first line on each side. Cut off the two corners to form a triangular gable. Repeat with one more rectangular piece.

Assemble the house by placing one of the square pieces flat on your work surface. Place the other two square pieces on either side of the base and the two gable pieces on each end. Nail into place.

The next step is to make the roof: Cut a $1\frac{1}{4}$-inch strip from the long side of one of the 5 × 6-inch rectangles. This will leave two pieces, one measuring $1\frac{1}{4}$" × 6" and the other, $4\frac{3}{4}$" × 6". Put the two pieces back together and attach the hinge in the center, as shown below. Nail the last rectangle to the hinged rectangle to form the roof. Place the roof on top of the house and adjust it to fit. Nail the un-hinged side of the roof to the walls and nail the top strip of the hinged side of the roof to each gable end. Leave the large part of the hinged side free so that it will open and close.

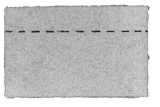

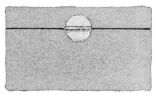

Paint the post office with exterior enamel to weatherproof it and decorate it as you wish. Instead of cutting an entrance hole as you would for a birdhouse, paint one on or paint on a door if you want it to look like a house or cabin. For further decoration, craft sticks can be glued or stapled on for a picket fence, twigs can be glued on to make a log cabin effect, pinecone "petals" can be glued on the roof to look like shingles, flowers and vines can be painted on to resemble a cottage.

If you want to have "signal flags," glue one end of each ribbon to a top edge of the inside of the box; pull the ribbon to the outside to flutter in the breeze and signal that there is a message inside for your friend. Each friend should have a different color ribbon.

Set the post office in a thick hedge, as Laurie did, or hang it from a branch or nail it in a sheltered spot.

Place a small notepad and pencil inside the post office so that you and your friends can write notes and leave them for each other. You'll want to check the post office regularly for messages!

Meg's Fringed Tea Cloth and Napkin Set

So a tray was fitted out before anyone began, and taken up, with the cook's compliments.

—Little Women, *Chapter Eleven*

"Fitting out" a tray, whether for serving breakfast to Marmee, as the girls were doing here, or for serving afternoon tea, required a tea cloth and napkins as well as china and silverware. The tea cloth was spread on the tray and was not only ornamental—it also kept the china from slipping around on the tray while it was carried from the kitchen and caught drops of tea or milk that might spill. A napkin, of course, was given to each guest although ladies of that day were trained to eat and drink so delicately, they hardly ever needed to use their napkins!

Today, we use paper napkins and placemats for everyday convenience, but for special occasions, it is much nicer to use linen or cotton ones, such as this easy-to-make set.

You will need:

$^2/_3$ yard linen or heavy cotton
Scissors
Iron

Cut out one piece of fabric 10" × 20"; cut four pieces 10" × 10" each.

Cut a $^1/_2$-inch square from each corner of all the pieces. Pull threads from all sides of the fabric to make a fringe about $^1/_2$ inch wide. At each corner, tie the end threads together to prevent further raveling.

With a heated iron, press the large cloth flat; fold each napkin into quarters and press.

To set up a tea tray, spread the large cloth on the tray. Set the teapot, cream and sugar, a small plate of lemon slices, cups and saucers, napkins, teaspoons, and a plate of cookies or other teatime treats on the tray—you may need *two* trays! A small vase of flowers will add the perfect finishing touch. Pass a napkin with each cup and saucer as you serve the tea.

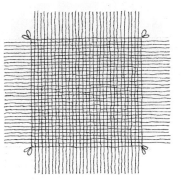

Amy's Acorn Tea Set

"I haven't heard Frank laugh so much for ever so long," said Grace to Amy, as they sat discussing dolls, and making tea-sets out of the acorn-cups.

—Little Women, *Chapter Twelve*

In honor of his friends, the Vaughns, who were visiting from England, Laurie had arranged a day of picnicking and games at Longmeadow, a little way up the river. The March girls, of course, were invited to come, along with Sallie Gardiner, Ned Moffat, and Laurie's tutor, John Brooke.

While the others talked, played croquet, and rode horses, twelve-year-old Amy and ten-year-old Grace Vaughn "became very good friends" and spent part of their day at "Camp Laurence" making tea sets from acorns they found under the trees.

Why not spend a pleasant summer afternoon making your own acorn tea set and serve "tea" to all your dolls?

Begin by collecting acorns, pinecones, nutshells, seed pods, tiny twigs, leaves, and other natural materials. Larger leaves can serve as trays, small leaves as plates. In order to fashion teacups from acorns, remove the acorn caps, use the caps as saucers, and use the acorns for cups. Hollow acorns can be filled with white sand for sugar and cream. Make a teapot from a flat-bottomed pinecone on which you can glue twigs or vine tendrils for handle and spout. Tiny twigs can also be used for spoons. For a bowl of berries to serve with the dolls' "tea," fill half a nutshell with tiny seeds or berries. A dried milk-weed pod with a few flower blossoms in it would make a fine centerpiece.

To make the leaf "tray" and "plates" last longer, press them between two sheets of waxed paper with a warm iron, removing the paper immediately. Leaves will have a light coating of wax that will keep them from drying out. Arrange the tea set on a shelf or dolls' table so that it will be ready for tea parties at any time.

FOR A DAY ON "DELECTABLE MOUNTAIN"

Each wore a large, flapping hat, a brown linen pouch slung over one shoulder, and carried a long staff. Meg had a cushion, Jo a book, Beth a basket, and Amy a portfolio.

—Little Women, *Chapter Thirteen*

The March girls were on an outing to "Delectable Mountain," a hill that rose steeply behind their house and which they had named in honor of one of the landmarks from their treasured *Pilgrim's Progress.* They settled themselves in a grove of pines on the hilltop and began their afternoon of "work and nice times." While they worked, they could admire the beautiful landscape and "look far away and see the country where we hope to live sometime."

Meg's Cushion

Meg sat upon her cushion, sewing daintily with her white hands and looking as fresh and sweet as a rose in her pink dress among the green.

—Little Women, *Chapter Thirteen*

Since Meg planned to spend her day on the "mountain" sewing, she wisely brought along a cushion to make her more comfortable. It would also help keep her dress from becoming soiled and damp as she sat on the grass.

Here is how to make a cushion for yourself such as the one Meg had.

> 2 18-inch squares of sturdy fabric (Meg would have loved a pretty rose-patterned chintz)
> Pins, needle, and thread
> Pillow stuffing

Pin the squares of fabric so that the right sides face each other and the wrong sides face you. Stitch all around about $1/2$ inch from the edge, leaving about a 5-inch opening on one side. Remove the pins, clip the corners, and press the seams open. Turn the pillow cover inside out; stuff it until the cushion is nice and plump. Pin the opening closed and stitch it securely.

Meg loved to add decorative touches to things she made and might have added a tassel to each corner of her cushion or some fringe around the edge.

Jo's Book Cover

Jo was knitting as she read aloud.
—Little Women, *Chapter Thirteen*

Jo loved the world of language and ideas. It seems that when she wasn't reading, she was writing, and when she wasn't writing, she was reading! She took a book along with her wherever she went and on the outing to "Delectable Mountain" she read aloud to her sisters while she knitted a sock.

Why not make a book cover to protect one of your favorite books if you like to carry it with you on outings as Jo did?

You will need:

A piece of heavy paper, such as pretty gift wrap or even wallpaper, about 3 inches wider on all sides than your *open* book
Scissors
Clear tape

Spread the paper, right side down, on a work surface. Open your book flat and place it on the paper so that there are about 3 inches of paper showing all around the edges of the book.

Carefully cut out a "V" above and below the book's spine. (You may want to mark this with a pencil first and remove the book before you cut the paper.)

Fold the top edges over the tops of the front and back book covers; do the same with the bottom edges. Fold over the side edges; crease the corners and fold them inside. Secure the flaps with tape, making sure you place the tape so that it sticks only to the paper cover, not to the book itself.

To make a coordinating bookmark, select a piece of ribbon to match one of the colors of your book cover. Cut it 3 inches longer than your book. Fold up a half inch or so at one end and stitch a small button to it. Cut a "V" in the other end of the ribbon.

You will have to teach *yourself* to read aloud and knit socks at the same time!

Beth's Gathering Basket and Pinecone Frame

Beth [had] a basket . . . and was sorting the cones that lay thick under the hemlock near by, for she made pretty things of them.
—Little Women, *Chapter Thirteen*

Beth was the homebody of the four girls and loved to make things for her family and friends. On their outing to "Delectable Mountain," she carried a basket for collecting cones, which she would later make up into "pretty things."

To make your own gathering basket, you will need:

A handled basket at least 10
    inches in diameter and a
    few inches deep
2 yards medium-to-wide satin
    or grosgrain ribbon
Ivy or wild grapevines
    (optional)
Pine needles, moss, or dry
    grass (optional)

Tie one end of the ribbon into a pretty bow around one end of the handle where it meets the basket. Wind the long end of the ribbon around and

around the handle until you get to the other end. Adjust the wound ribbon if necessary so that you have about 18 inches of ribbon left with which to tie another bow at the base of the handle.

If you like, twine ivy or wild grapevines around the handle, tucking the ends into the basket or under the ribbon to hold them in place.

Line the bottom of the basket with pine needles, moss, or dry grass if you wish.

Gather an assortment of cones and arrange them in the basket. You will begin to notice that there are many shapes and sizes of cones. Some cones are very tiny, less than an inch long; others are huge, about the size of a football! There are long, thin ones; short, fat ones; closed and open ones.

A basket of dried cones by the hearth is charming in fall and winter; the cones can be used as kindling if desired.

MAKING "PRETTY THINGS" OF YOUR CONES:

Cones can be made into beautiful decorations, from Christmas tree ornaments to wreaths and picture frames. We are not told exactly what Beth made of hers, except that she made "pretty things of them." Perhaps she made the frame for one of Demi's pictures that Nat noticed on his first night at Plumfield:

There were several others on the walls, but the boy thought there must be something peculiar about this one, for it had a graceful frame of moss and cones about it, and on a little bracket underneath stood a vase of wild flowers freshly gathered from the spring woods.

— Little Men, *Chapter Three*

Here is one way to make your own frame of moss and cones:

> 1 unfinished wood picture
>   frame with flat surfaces (or
>   make a frame from heavy
>   cardboard)
> Assorted evergreen cones
> Sheet moss or Spanish moss
>   twigs, lichens, other
>   natural materials (optional)
> Glue

Arrange cones (and other materials) on the frame in the design of your choice and glue in place. Let the frame lie on a flat surface until the glue is dry.

Place a pretty picture in the frame. Display it on the wall or prop it up on a bookshelf.

Amy's Portfolio

"I have ever so many wishes, but the pet one is to be an artist, and go to Rome, and do fine pictures, and be the best artist in the whole world" was Amy's modest desire.

—Little Women, *Chapter Thirteen*

Amy practiced her drawing and sketching on her outings with her sisters. She always took a sketch pad and pencils with her and carried her finished sketches in a portfolio to protect them. It's easy to make one for yourself.

You will need:

> 2 pieces lightweight
>   cardboard, about
>   16" × 18" each
> 2-inch-wide (or wider) tape
> Hole punch
> 2 18-inch pieces of narrow
>   ribbon

Place the two pieces of cardboard side by side lengthwise. Tape them together, running the tape lengthwise so that half of the tape is on one piece of cardboard and half is on the other piece. Turn the hinged pieces over and tape them down the same way on the other side so that you have a sturdy hinge.

If you wish, cover the portfolio with pretty fabric or heavy paper.

Make a hole in the center of each long unhinged side, about a half inch from the edge. Run one piece of ribbon through the holes and tie it in a bow to hold the portfolio together. Tie your sketching pencils together with the second piece of ribbon.

Now you are ready to fill your portfolio with pretty sketches of flowers and ferns as Amy did.

Beth's Pressed Pansy Pictures

"Dear Mother,—
"There is only room for me to send my love, and some pressed pansies . . ."
"Little Beth"

—Little Women, *Chapter Sixteen*

Pressing flowers was a favorite activity of Victorian times. Many ladies made pictures with them. Every flower had a "meaning," too—roses meant "love," for example, and pansies meant "thoughts." The pansies that Beth sent to Marmee while she was caring for Mr. March in the hospital were not only a little gift from home—they were one more indication that Beth's thoughts were with her mother and father while they were away.

Here is how to make your own "thoughtful" picture:

Pick several fresh pansies and a few of their leaves. In the back pages of a large book, such as a telephone book or a dictionary, place the pansies and leaves facedown and press them gently with your fingers to flatten them slightly. Close the book carefully and do not disturb it for at least twenty-four hours.

Once the flowers and leaves are pressed, carefully arrange them in a pretty design on a card of heavy paper. Glue them in place with tiny drops of glue, just enough to hold them. If you like, you can add stems, tendrils, and other embellishments with colored pencils or pens.

Pressed flowers can decorate all kinds of things—place cards, paper placemats, stationery, greeting cards, picture frames, bookmarks, or book covers.

112

Amy's Grand Tour Folder

"Oh, I can't begin to tell you how I enjoy it all! I never can, so I'll only give you bits out of my notebook, for I've done nothing but sketch and scribble since I started."

—Little Women, *Chapter Thirty-one*

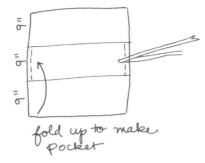

fold up to make pocket

Amy was in Europe! She had been invited to go with Aunt Carrol and her daughter, Flo, on an extensive tour that would take them to Ireland, England, France, Germany, Switzerland, and Italy.

Amy kept her sketchbook, pencils, notebook, and stationery close at hand during her travels so that she could capture a scene or a thought at just the right moment. Here is a useful accessory that will help to keep your notebook and other items ready for your own trips, short or long.

You will need:

18" × 27" heavy cotton fabric
Needle and thread
Chalk
48-inch length of grosgrain
　　ribbon

Begin by hemming all four edges of the fabric. Then lay the fabric right side down and fold up the bottom third of fabric to form a pocket 8 to 9 inches deep. Pin in place.

Fold 18 inches of the ribbon down and insert the folded end of the ribbon, into the right side of the pocket, $4\frac{1}{2}$ inches from the bottom of the folder, as shown. Pin in place. Two lengths of ribbon should extend out from the right side of the pocket; the top piece should be 30 inches long and the bottom piece should be the 18-inch length you folded down previously.

Stitch the left and right sides of the pocket closed about $\frac{1}{4}$ inch from the edges.

From the stitching, measure 5 inches in from each side and mark with a chalk line. Stitch down the lines to form three pockets, two 5-inch-wide side pockets and one 6-inch-wide center pocket.

Insert a 6" × 8" notepad in the center pocket, postcards and a pen in the right pocket, and a map or other items in the left pocket.

Fold the top flap over the pocket end, then fold in thirds, starting with the left side and ending with right side on top. Wrap the long end of the ribbon around the travel folder and tie with the other end in a bow.

Bon voyage!

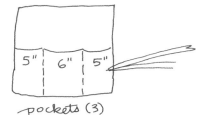

pockets (3)

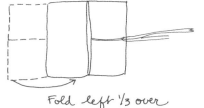

Fold left ⅓ over

Fold right ⅓ over and tie

Jo's Sausage Pillow

Among the many pillows that adorned the venerable couch was one, hard, round, covered with prickly horsehair and furnished with a knobby button at each end.

—Little Women, *Chapter Thirty-two*

There were many pillows on the Marches' old parlour sofa. Jo used the so-called sausage pillow as "a weapon of defence, a barricade, or a stern preventive of too much slumber." She also used it to signal Laurie whether or not she wanted company—if she had stood the pillow "on an end," he could feel free to sit beside her, but if she had placed the pillow flat, Laurie knew she did not want to be disturbed.

Louisa May Alcott herself had a sausage pillow that she used in much the same way Jo did. She called it her "mood" pillow.

To make a sausage pillow of your own, you will need:

1 piece sturdy fabric,
    about 17" × 23"
Needle and thread
1 bag pillow stuffing
2 large buttons, $1\frac{1}{2}$ inches
    to 2 inches in diameter

With a needle and thread, sew a line of basting stitches $\frac{1}{2}$ inch from each 17-inch edge of the fabric. Leave about 2 inches of thread extending at each end of the line of stitches.

Fold the fabric, right sides together, and stitch the two 23-inch edges together with a $\frac{1}{2}$-inch seam allowance. Press the seam open.

Pull the basting stitches on one end of the tube to gather the material tightly. Tie the ends of the thread together in a knot; stitch the gathers together at the center to hold them closed securely. Turn the tube right side out and fill tightly with pillow stuffing to within $2\frac{1}{2}$ inches of the top.

Pull the gathers at the open end together firmly, tie the threads in a knot, and tuck the raw edges inside. Stitch the opening closed.

Sew a button at each end of the pillow to cover the gathered centers.

Autograph-Seekers' Album

"You can leave your albums and have them sent when Mrs. Bhaer has written a sentiment in 'em."

—Jo's Boys, *Chapter Three*

Although Jo discontinued her "scribbling" for a few years while she and Professor Bhaer were organizing their school, she picked up her pen again when extra money was needed and "a book for girls" was "wanted by a certain publisher." She wrote "a little story describing a few scenes and adventures in the lives of herself and her sisters" and it was a phenomenal success. Jo became quite a famous author and was besieged by admirers who wanted her to write in their autograph books, a fad among young people at the time.

Here's how to make a simple autograph album for your own friends to write "sentiments" in for you to treasure. You will need:

25 4" × 6" white or pastel unlined index cards

1 4" × 6" picture postcard or greeting card

$\frac{1}{8}$-inch satin cord (about 12 inches long) with tassels at each end (purchase this at a fabric or craft shop)

$\frac{1}{4}$-inch hole punch

Punch a hole in the top left-hand corner of each card, about $\frac{1}{2}$ inch from the edges. Stack the cards so that the holes are aligned. Place the postcard on top of the stack of cards as a front cover.

Fold the tasseled cord in half and insert the folded end through the holes in the stack of cards. Loop the end of the cord over the tassels and pull snugly against the cards to hold them in place.

Have your friends write a short message on each card. They should sign their names and write the date, too. If a famous person happens to visit, perhaps he or she will sign your autograph book!

Display your autograph album either closed or fanned out so that the messages can be viewed. You can easily add more blank cards to your book as you need them.

A Plumfield Nature Corner

"I've been thinking that it would be a good plan for you fellows to have a museum of your own: a place in which to collect all the curious and interesting things that you find and make, and have given you."

—Little Men, *Chapter Eleven*

The boys and girls at Jo and Professor Bhaer's Plumfield School loved to collect all sorts of things they found while wandering in the woods and fields around Plumfield. Wasps' nests, snakeskins, unusual rocks, feathers, birds' eggs, and other treasures were displayed in their own museum, the old carriage house Laurie had fixed up for the purpose.

You don't need a carriage house to have a little museum of your own.

Select a table or shelf on which to display the treasures you find in your own yard, a city park, or as you walk on nature trails or along a beach. You are sure to find empty birds' nests, feathers, unusual stones, beetle shells, wildflowers, seed pods, lichens, seashells, arrowheads, and other items. You may not be allowed to remove some of these things from certain areas, so be sure to check first; perhaps making a snapshot of them would be a way to include them in your collection. Amy, of course, would have carried her sketchbook and pencils with her so that she could sketch any interesting objects she came across during her walks; you can do this, too.

Clean up your treasures before you bring them into the house. Make a card for each item you find, writing the name of the item, the date, and the place you found it. Write any other interesting facts that you discover about it on the card. Put the card in a file box nearby. You may also want to make a small label for each item you display.

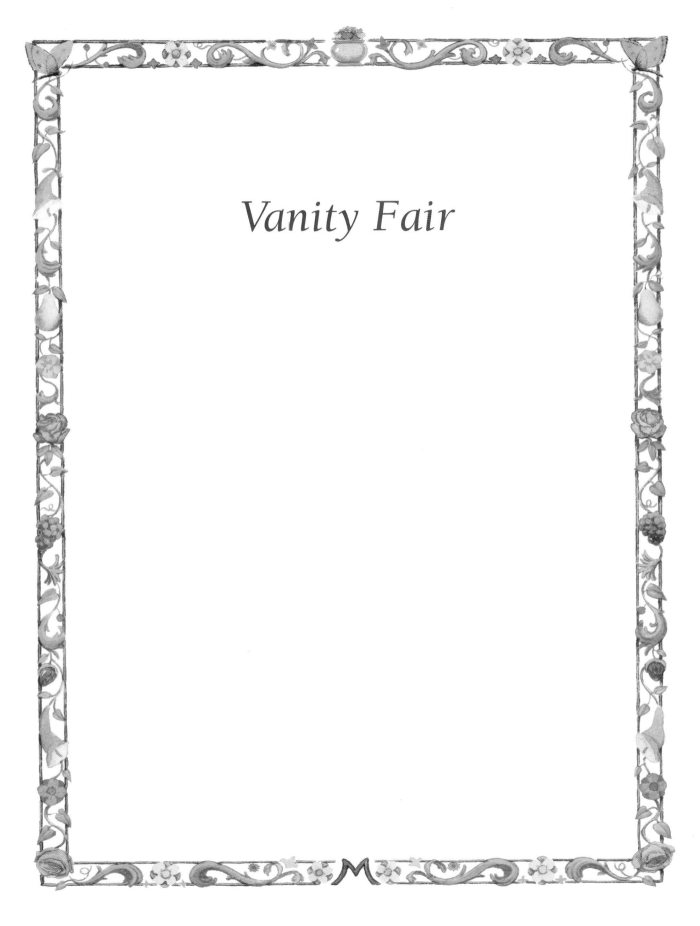

Vanity Fair

Fashions from the
Little Women Era

When the evening for the "small party" came, she found that the
poplin wouldn't do at all, for the other girls were putting on thin
dresses and making themselves very fine indeed. . . .
                                        —Little Women, *Chapter Nine*

"Vanity Fair" was one stop on the Pilgrim's Progress to the Celestial City. At the Fair, all kinds of vanities were sold to tempt the pilgrims—"houses, lands, trades, places, honors, preferments, titles," as well as "silver, gold, pearls, precious stones," to name but a few.

Beth and Jo did not tarry too long at "Vanity Fair," for neither of them cared much for fashion or appearances. But Meg and Amy found their feet dragging as they made their way along this part of the pilgrim's way.

Meg accepted her friend Belle's offer to make her into "a little beauty" for the Moffats' party. She was dressed in a fancy dress, given jewelry to wear, silk boots, "a plumy fan, and a bouquet in a silver holder." This was a radical departure from her own "dowdy tarlatan," which she had worn the night before, and, while she was amazed and gratified by the reflection in her mirror, she also felt "queer and stiff and half-dressed." She ended the evening with the "feeling that she had been to a masquerade, and hadn't enjoyed herself as much as she expected."

Marmee listened to her story the next evening and gave her this advice: "Learn to know and value the praise which is worth having, and to excite the admiration of excellent people by being modest as well as pretty, Meg." With this advice, Meg left "Vanity Fair" to continue her "journey" with a much lighter burden.

Amy found "Vanity Fair" even more difficult to resist than Meg. She loved pretty clothes and fine things and found being "poor" very inconvenient. She vowed to marry a rich man one day.

Clothing styles, especially for women, were very different in the *Little Women* era than they are today. The most important concern for women at that time was to be modest; to show one's ankles, legs, or bare arms was considered very bad taste. Bright colors, strong patterns, or any trimmings that called too much attention to the wearer were also frowned upon.

In 1860, the year *Little Women* begins, women wore dresses with long, full skirts and fitted bodices with long sleeves and high necklines. Daytime dresses were made of wool or cotton; for special occasions, dresses of silk were the most fashionable. The March girls, however, were too poor to consider having silk dresses and had to be satisfied with their poplins, tarlatans, and organdies for parties. (Louisa herself had always longed for a silk dress, but she did not have one until she was twenty-four years old. Her cousin gave it to her for a Christmas gift.)

Underneath their skirts, fashionable women wore hoops that made the skirts stand out all around, as well as several long petticoats. To make their waists appear as tiny as possible, women wore corsets with long, thin whalebone stays that were sewn into them; these corsets were laced up quite tightly. The lacing and the stays not only shaped the figure but also insured that the wearer would stand and sit up absolutely straight. Camisoles (sleeveless cotton undershirts) were worn over and under the corset. The first camisole protected the skin from the chafing of the corset and the outer camisole covered the corset, protecting the fabric of the bodice.

After the Civil War, the fashionable silhouette changed dramatically. Wide skirts narrowed and the fullness was gathered in the back. Bustles were worn instead of hoops to make skirts stand out even more in back. Not until the turn of the century did a more natural silhouette become fashionable. Long skirts, however, were worn until the 1920s, when the "flapper" era of short skirts and sleeveless blouses changed women's clothes— and attitudes—forever.

There were also many accessories without which a woman's ensemble of the *Little Women* era would have been incomplete. Marmee taught the girls that "a real lady is always known by neat boots, gloves, and handkerchief." Boots were usually made of soft leather, came about two inches above the ankle, and were laced or buttoned with tiny shoe-buttons. Gloves, made of soft kidskin, were "more important than anything else,"

according to Meg as she reminds Jo before the Gardiners' New Year's Eve party. The gloves must be perfectly clean, too, to be respectable. A clean white pocket handkerchief was also essential. The March girls could expect a reminder from Marmee about this each time they left the house—"Girls, girls! *have* you both got nice pocket-handkerchiefs?" she cries from a window as Meg and Jo leave for the New Year's Eve party.

In addition to boots, gloves, and handkerchiefs, ladies always wore hats when they went out during the day. Hats protected their faces from the sun and their hair from the dust of the unpaved roads. Sometimes ladies carried parasols as an additional shield from the bright sun.

Nearly everything people wore in those days, from dresses to underwear, was homemade or made by a tailor or dressmaker. Sewing machines, though invented in 1840, were rare until after the Civil War and even then were not yet common appliances in most households. The long seams and hems of the women's voluminous skirts and petticoats, as well as all the sheets and blankets for the family, were sewn by hand; ruffles, flounces, tucks, and other trimmings were also handsewn.

Jo was the chief dressmaker for the March family. Although she didn't care much for stylish fashions—she preferred to be "neat and cool and comfortable" and to be in the company of people who liked her for herself rather than for her clothes—she did pride herself on her skill with a needle:

At that minute Jo was particularly absorbed in dressmaking; for she was mantua-maker general to the family, and took especial credit to herself because she could use a needle as well as a pen.

Like Jo, Louisa was a good seamstress; for years she earned her living sewing for other people. It was not until she was thirty-one years old that Louisa began to earn enough money from writing that she could put aside her sewing jobs, yet she continued to make many clothes for herself and her family. Unlike Jo, however, Louisa enjoyed pretty clothes and, once she began to earn enough money, indulged herself in the fashionable attire so long denied her.

Roses and
Snowdrops

Gardens, Flowers, and Related Activities from the *Little Women* Books

The June roses over the porch were awake bright and early on that morning, rejoicing with all their hearts in the cloudless sunshine, like friendly little neighbors, as they were.

—Little Women, *Chapter Twenty-five*

From the flowerbeds of the March home to the orchards of Plumfield, plants of all kinds played an important role in the lives of the "little women." In the spring, the snowdrops and daffodils signaled the end of the long winter. Soon, the apple trees, sweet peas, lilies of the valley, and June roses began to bloom. Annuals were planted and tended for summer bouquets along with herbs and vegetables for the table. The golden weeks of autumn meant days of apple picking and gathering the remainder of the harvest from the garden—pumpkins, carrots, turnips, potatoes to store away for winter, as well as great bouquets of goldenrod, asters, bright leaves, and dried grasses for the house. Even in winter, the Marches continued to indulge their love of gardening. In the first chapter of *Little Women*, "chrysanthemums and Christmas roses bloomed in the windows" of the Marches' parlour, lending a cheerful and luxurious note to an otherwise simply furnished room. Windows served as little greenhouses in the winter, and windowsills held not only chrysanthemums and roses but also pansies, hyacinths, snowdrops, and geraniums. The Laurences next door had a "conservatory"—a heated glass room in which flowers and plants could grow all year. Old Mr. Laurence sent "four great bouquets of hot-house flowers" from this conservatory to the March girls along with the refreshments on Christmas night.

Most houses of that era had a kitchen garden in which the family would grow vegetables and herbs for their own use and sometimes enough to sell at the town market. We are not told much about the Marches' kitchen garden but we know that the Alcotts had a great garden and an orchard on their twelve-acre property in Concord. Mr. Alcott tried to grow as much of his family's food as possible. The family grew several varieties of apples—Baldwins, Sweetings, Northern Spies, and golden pippins. They also grew beets, parsnips, turnips, tomatoes, and other vegetables. Strawberries lined the path to the summer house on the hill and a hops vine climbed over one of the porches. Mrs. Alcott made beer from the ripened hops. Just down the road from Orchard House lived Ephraim Bull, who was responsible for developing the famous Concord grape; he gave some of his grapevines to the Alcotts for their garden.

The March girls, however, were more interested in their flower garden on the east side of the house, which they could look out on from the parlour, dining room, kitchen, and two upstairs bedrooms. A "low hedge" grew behind the garden along the boundary between the Marches' and the Laurences' "estates"; this is where Laurie set the birdhouse "post-office" for the two households to exchange gifts and messages.

The Marches' flower garden provided bouquets for the house in the summer and fall (it was Jo's responsibility to "keep the vases filled") and, of course, the June roses and lilies of the valley for Meg's wedding. The girls often picked flowers from the garden to wear on their dresses or in their hair, for Marmee thought "real flowers were the prettiest ornament for a young girl."

There were other gardens in the *Little Women* books—Meg's garden at the Dove-cote, the orchards and vegetable gardens at Plumfield, and the unforgettable European gardens that Amy and Laurie strolled through in Nice and Vevey.

You can grow some of the same plants that Meg, Jo, Beth, and Amy loved and use them as they did—in bouquets, nosegays, floral wreaths, and in many other ways. Whether you choose to plant an entire garden with all of their favorite flowers, a single hanging basket with a few favorites, or simply one or two hyacinth bulbs on a sunny windowsill, you will be re-creating a bit of the world of *Little Women* for yourself.

THE MARCH GIRLS' GARDEN

The garden had to be put in order, and each sister had a quarter of the little plot to do what she liked with.

—Little Women, *Chapter Ten*

Of the girls' garden plots, Hannah said, "I'd know which each of them gardings belonged to, ef I see 'em in Chiny" because they so perfectly re-flected each girl's personality. Meg chose refined flowers such as roses

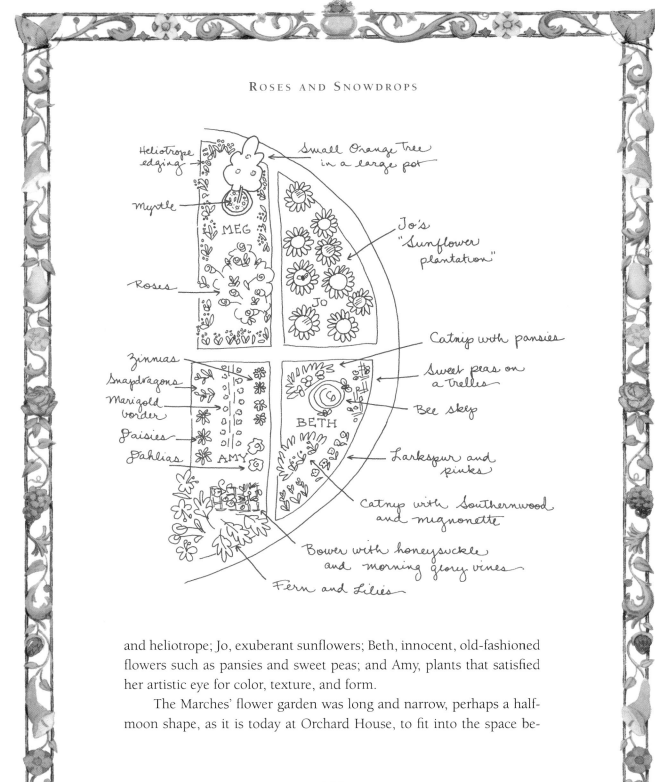

Heliotrope edging

Small Orange Tree in a large pot

Myrtle

MEG

Jo's "Sunflower plantation"

Roses

JO

Catnip with pansies

Zinnias

Sweet peas on a trellis

Snapdragons

Marigold border

Bee skep

BETH

Daisies

Dahlias

AMY

Larkspur and pinks

Catnip with Southernwood and mignonette

Bower with honeysuckle and morning glory vines

Fern and Lilies

and heliotrope; Jo, exuberant sunflowers; Beth, innocent, old-fashioned flowers such as pansies and sweet peas; and Amy, plants that satisfied her artistic eye for color, texture, and form.

The Marches' flower garden was long and narrow, perhaps a half-moon shape, as it is today at Orchard House, to fit into the space between the house and the property line. There were paths marking off each girl's quarter.

Choose a sunny spot for your flower garden. Decide on a shape and size that is in keeping with your space. Choose which plants you want in your garden and which ones will grow best—perhaps you have room for only some of the plants the March girls grew; perhaps you have more shade than they did. You may have to adjust and substitute different flowers; if so, consider yourself another Jo—be experimental!

Sketch a plan for the garden on paper, then in your garden plot, mark off the paths and beds with small wooden stakes and string. With a spade, dig the edges of the paths and then dig out the sod to make the paths. Put the sod and dirt you dig from the paths into the garden beds.

Dig up each bed, breaking up clods of dirt and sod, mixing them into the beds; add compost, peat moss, and some fertilizer to condition the soil.

Spread the paths with hay, bark mulch, or gravel to keep them from turning to mud when it rains.

Here are some ideas for planting each of the March girls' garden plots, along with some of the ways in which they used their flowers.

• Meg's Garden •

Meg's had roses and heliotrope, myrtle, and a little orange tree in it.

—Little Women, *Chapter Ten*

For Meg's quarter, plant one or several rosebushes in the center of the plot. Meg would have planted an old-fashioned, hardy variety such as Rosa rugosa, a pretty pink rose. Dig the hole for the roses deep and mix in some fertilizer before setting the rosebush in. Water the plants well. Plant heliotrope around the edges of the plot. Set a "small orange tree" in a pot and underplant it with sprigs of myrtle, also known as vinca, a low-growing ground cover with tiny blue flowers. Place the potted orange tree in a corner of the plot. Orange trees are not hardy in cold climates, so you will need to bring your plant inside during cold weather. It will need a very sunny window and frequent watering and misting.

FLOWER ARRANGING WITH MEG

Feeling almost happy again, she laid by a few ferns and roses for herself and quickly made up the rest in dainty bouquets for the breasts, hair, or skirts of her friends, offering them so prettily that Clara, the older sister, told her she was "the sweetest little thing she ever saw," and they looked quite charmed with her small attention.

—Little Women, *Chapter Nine*

Meg was feeling quite sorry for herself as she prepared for the Moffats' party. All the other girls were wearing much finer party dresses than she could ever hope to have. Then a box arrived from Laurie, filled with roses, heath, and ferns, creating a sensation among the girls and a feeling of gratitude in Meg. She shared the flowers with the other girls, impressing them even more with her generosity and skill at arranging the flowers in "dainty bouquets."

Arrange your own bouquets from flowers you receive or grow in your garden. They can be as dainty as Meg's party bouquets, with a few flowers and leaves in a small cluster, or as showy as the Christmas bouquet of red roses, white chrysanthemums, and trailing vines (page 143).

For a dainty bouquet or "nosegay," surround an open or half-open rose with rosebuds and heath (or baby's breath, if you prefer). Place small fern fronds or other "feathery" greenery all around the outside of the bouquet. Wrap florist's tape around the stems or simply twist a rubber band around them to hold them in place. Wind a pretty ribbon around the stems, tie it in a bow, and let the ends of the ribbon trail prettily.

Carry the nosegay, pin it to your waistband, or wear it in your hair.

You can also place dainty bouquets in small vases and set them on tea tables or tea trays or even your dressing table.

· Jo's Garden ·

Jo's bed was never alike in two seasons, for she was always trying experiments. This year it was to be a plantation of sunflowers, the seeds of which cheerful and aspiring plant were to feed "Aunt Cockle-top" and her family of chicks.

—Little Women, *Chapter Ten*

Jo's "sunflower plantation" is easy to grow. Just scatter sunflower seeds over the garden plot and cover them lightly with a layer of soil. Water them well. They will grow fast. Some sunflowers are short but most are tall and will soon grow to be taller than you are.

JO'S SUNFLOWER UMBRELLA HOUSE

Jo . . . looked up at him with an expression that plainly showed how happy she would be to walk through life beside him, even though she had no better shelter than the old umbrella, if he carried it.

—Little Women, *Chapter Forty-six*

In honor of both Jo's sunflowers and Professor Bhaer's umbrella that played such an important role later in her life, create a little sunflower "umbrella house" in your garden.

Plant some of the sunflower seeds in a circle about two or three feet in diameter. When the sunflowers are tall enough, gather the stalks near the top

135

and loosely tie them together with twine or raffia. This will provide a shady, sheltered spot in which to sit and write your own stories or make into a playhouse. You might want to furnish your "sunflower umbrella house" with a little bench—Jo surely would have added one to her plot so that she would have an inviting place to write on sunny days.

• Beth's Garden •

Beth had old-fashioned, fragrant flowers in her garden—sweet peas and mignonette, larkspur, pinks, pansies, and southernwood, with chickweed for the bird and catnip for the pussies.
—Little Women, *Chapter Ten*

The fragrant flowers in Beth's plot would have been attractive to bees and butterflies and even hummingbirds so you might want to consider making a bird feeder, birdbath, or a "bee skep" the centerpiece of this plot. Put the taller plants, such as the larkspur and pinks, at the back of the garden; let the sweet peas climb up a trellis (you can purchase one at a garden store). Plant the lower-growing flowers, such as mignonette, pansies, southernwood, chickweed, and catnip, in front.

BETH'S GARDEN PARTY FOR HER DOLLS

There were six dolls to be taken up and dressed every morning, for Beth was a child still, and loved her pets as well as ever.
—Little Women, *Chapter Four*

It is likely that Beth took her dolls out into the garden for tea parties in fine weather, for she liked to

136

take them outside "to breathe the air," and you can, too. Set up your doll furniture in or near your garden (or spread a little cloth on the grass if you prefer). Decorate the tabletop or picnic cloth with leaves arranged in a pretty design. Gather a few flowers from your garden for a center-piece.

Did you make Amy's Acorn Tea Set (page 107)? If so, this would be the perfect occasion to bring it out. Serve your dolls a tiny version of Daisy's Patty-Cake Cookies (page 86) or make a little plate of pretend cookies with flower petals. Perhaps a little sparrow or a kitten will join you for your tea party, especially if you have planted a bit of chickweed or catnip in your garden.

• Amy's Garden •

Amy had a bower in hers—rather small and earwiggy, but very pretty to look at—with honeysuckles and morning glories hanging their colored horns and bells in graceful wreaths all over it; tall, white lilies, delicate ferns, and as many brilliant, picturesque plants as would consent to blossom there.

—Little Women, *Chapter Ten*

You can purchase a ready-made arch of lattice or you can fashion your own from small branches or wild grapevines, and twine or wire. Push the lower ends of the bower about twelve inches into the ground. Plant honeysuckle and morning glory vines at the base of the bower. Soon they will begin to grow up the sides and over the top, "hanging their col-ored horns and bells in graceful wreaths all over it." Around the bower, plant "tall, white lilies," such as Madonna lilies, and "delicate ferns." You can also choose "as many brilliant, picturesque plants" to place in Amy's plot as you like, such as daisies, snapdragons, marigolds, zinnias, and dianthus.

AMY'S ARTISTIC HANGING BASKETS

The evergreen arch wouldn't stay firm after she got it up, but wiggled and threatened to tumble down on her head when the hanging baskets were filled . . .

—Little Women, *Chapter Thirty*

Amy was honored to have been invited to preside over the prestigious art table at Mrs. Chester's "fair," an event Mrs. Chester organized to raise funds for the freedmen after the War. However, due to a misunderstanding, Amy was asked, at the last minute, to take the flower table instead and the art table was given to May, Mrs. Chester's daughter.

Although Amy was hurt by the sudden decision to replace her at the art table she had worked so hard on, she was determined not to let anyone know it. She vowed to do her best with the flower table even with its uncooperative evergreen arch! She finally secured the arch and hanging baskets and arranged the table prettily. Laurie and his friends came to the fair and bought all of her bouquets and baskets, making Amy's flower table the most successful display of the whole evening.

To make a hanging basket such as the ones Amy had at her flower table, line a wire hanging-basket form (you can purchase these at garden centers) with a thick layer of sheet moss. Fill the basket about two-thirds full of potting soil. Arrange a variety of flowering plants and vines in the soil and add enough potting soil to hold the plants securely in place. Water the basket thoroughly and hang it from a tree branch or perhaps in the center of your vine-covered arbor. Water the basket frequently, daily in hot weather, and fertilize it weekly.

Nasturtiums, fuchsias, ivy geraniums, petunias, pansies, impatiens, ivy, vinca vines, and asparagus ferns will make colorful and artistic hanging baskets.

BETH AND AMY'S FRESH FLOWER WREATH

Beth helped her dress, and made a charming little wreath for her hair.

—Little Women, *Chapter Thirty*

Amy had returned home after her trying afternoon at Mrs. Chester's fair, where she had been "demoted" from hosting the art table to hosting the flower table. Worse, she had to go back that evening! But Beth's flower wreath was a delightful addition to Amy's ensemble as well as a sweet reminder of her sister's gentle thoughtfulness.

To make your own flower wreath, collect about two dozen long-stemmed flowers such as daisies, Queen Anne's lace, or purple clover. Cut the stems to about six inches long and remove most of the lower leaves from the stems. Make a "rope" of the flowers by winding thread around the stems of three of the flowers at a time; add another bunch of three flowers about every three inches, tying them to the stems of the previous bunch. Tie the two ends of the floral rope together to fit around your head.

THE PLUMFIELD GARDEN

"These are our farms," said Tommy. "We each have our own patch, and raise what we like in it, only we have to choose different things, and can't change till the crop is in, and we must keep it in order all summer."

—Little Men, *Chapter Three*

The boys at Plumfield planted fruits and vegetables that they could sell to Professor Bhaer for pocket money. The professor turned the bounty over to Jo and Asia, the cook, to add to the ever-disappearing stores in the pantry.

Depending on how much room you have for a kitchen garden, select from the following Plumfield "crops" the ones you wish to grow:

Jack and Ned's potatoes
Emil and Franz's sweet corn and popcorn
Nat's beans
Tommy's peas
Demi's lettuces and turnips
Dick's carrots
Rob's squashes and pumpkins
Billy's cucumbers
Stuffy's melons

Nan's herb garden with a variety of herbs including parsley, rosemary, mint, chives, sage, or thyme can be planted with the flowers or vegetables or in a plot by itself. Or perhaps you would rather plant some of Daisy's flowers—roses, pansies, sweet peas, mignonette, larkspur, canary vine, snapdragons, poppies, and coreopsis. You can plant them in a flower box or a window box or a large container, whatever suits your own space.

• Demi's Floral Proposal •

"I read in one of Miss Edgeworth's stories about a man who offers three roses to his lady—a bud, a half-blown, and a full-blown rose. I don't remember which she took; but it's a pretty way; and Alice knows about it because she was there when we read it."

—Jo's Boys, *Chapter Nineteen*

The idea that there is a "language of flowers" was very popular in the Victorian age. Every flower had its own meaning and dictionaries were published so that everyone would know the meanings of the flowers. When a bouquet was sent, the recipient would appreciate not only the beauty of the flowers, but also the silent "message" they might carry. Pansies meant "thoughts"; lilies, "purity"; ivy, "friendship"; ferns, "sincerity"; violets, "faithfulness"; and daisies, "innocence." Perhaps the most frequently sent flowers were roses, for they were the flowers of "love." But roses of different colors meant different degrees of love, as did the stage of the flower. For instance, pink roses meant "love hopeful and expectant," red roses, "love triumphant," and white roses, such as the ones Demi sent Alice, signified "no other love." A rosebud would indicate "there is hope," a half-opened rose would mean "we must wait," and a fully opened rose would announce "I accept your proposal."

Demi's roses, which he stripped of every thorn to show that he would not willingly cause his beloved the slightest pain, were his marriage proposal—subtle, yet unmistakable in the "language of flowers." Alice gave her answer with those same roses that evening—she wore them over her heart.

· Jo's Autumn Bounty ·

She glorified the walls with yellow maple boughs and scarlet woodbine wreaths, or filled her vases with russet ferns, hemlock sprays full of delicate cones, and hardy autumn flowers. . . .

—Little Men, *Chapter Eighteen*

Jo celebrated autumn at Plumfield with her "little men" by having apple-picking festivals, complete with out-of-doors teas in the afternoon. She delighted in decorating the parlour and other rooms of the house with bouquets, wreaths, and garlands from the "woodland harvest" that Dan gathered in the fields and woods nearby. Dan brought "graceful seeded grasses, clematis tassels, downy soft yellow waxwork berries and mosses" by the armful along with the maple boughs, woodbine, ferns, hemlock sprays, and autumn flowers.

You can find all sorts of brightly colored leaves, grasses, berries, and ferns in the autumn, too, as well as fall flowers such as chrysanthemums, asters, goldenrod, and yarrow. Gather them into bunches and put them in vases to set on your mantel or tables, or tie them with raffia for a dramatic door decoration.

• Professor Bhaer's Winter Hyacinths •

He looked sober in spite of his humming, till he went to the window to turn the hyacinth bulbs toward the sun. . . .

—Little Women, *Chapter Thirty-three*

This was Jo's first good look at Professor Bhaer as she peeped through the curtain covering the glass door between the parlour and the nursery of her boarding house in New York. He "looked like a gentlemen" and intrigued Jo.

Louisa also grew hyacinths on her windowsill at Orchard House and when they bloomed in January of 1868, she considered them "a good omen." She was right—*Little Women* was published later that year.

Hyacinths can be planted in the fall outdoors to bloom with the tulips and daffodils the next spring or they can be "forced" to bloom much earlier so that you can enjoy their beauty and sweet fragrance in midwinter.

Buy your hyacinth bulbs in the fall. Hyacinths come in various shades of pink, white, or blue. If they have not been "pre-chilled" by the nursery, put the bulbs in a brown paper bag and put them in the lower part of your refrigerator to chill for at least three weeks.

Remove the bulbs from the refrigerator about six weeks before you want them to bloom and place each in a special hyacinth vase, if you have one, or in a pot or jar. If you are using a hyacinth vase, set one hyacinth bulb in the top portion of the vase and pour water in the bottom of the vase just until it touches the base of the bulb. (If the bulb itself sits in water, it will rot, but the roots of the bulb need to be in the water.) To plant the hyacinths in a pot or jar, fill the container about two-thirds full of small pebbles. Set the bulb (or bulbs) on top of the pebbles and add more pebbles to cover the bulbs about halfway up (the pebbles will help hold the bulbs in place, especially when they bloom). Add enough water to the container to come up just to the bases of the bulbs.

Check the container every day to keep the water at the right level and turn it a quarter- or a half-turn, as Professor Bhaer did, so that the stem will grow straight—if left in one position, the stem will bend toward the sun and the heavy flower will eventually fall over.

Once the roots start to grow, the top of the bulb will sprout green leaves, and then a stem with a large bud on top will emerge. In a few days, the bud will burst into bloom with many tiny flowerets massed together to form what looks like a single flower.

For an extra pretty touch, tie a ribbon around the vase or pot to match the color of the hyacinth blossom you planted.

A CHRISTMAS CENTERPIECE

There was a great deal of love done up in the few little bundles, and the tall vase of red roses, white chrysanthemums, and trailing vines, which stood in the middle, gave quite an elegant air to the table.

—Little Women, *Chapter Two*

This special Christmas arrangement, cut from their own houseplants, had decorated the Marches' dining room table but the girls carried it, along with their Christmas morning breakfast, to the poor Hummel family.

To make a similar centerpiece for your own Christmas table, you will need:

A tall vase (crystal or silver are prettiest with roses)
Three to six long-stemmed red roses
One or two large bunches of white chrysanthemums
Several stems of ivy, about 12 to 18 inches long
1 yard half-inch dark red velvet ribbon

Fill the vase about half full with warm water. Strip the leaves from the lower ends of the stems of the flowers and vines.

Arrange the chrysanthemums in the vase and add the roses, spaced evenly through the chrysanthemums. Arrange the stems of ivy around the edges of the vase so that they trail down the sides.

Weave the ribbon through the flowers. Set the vase on a lace doily or placemat to absorb any drops of water.

Change the water every few days to keep the flowers fresh.

A REMEMBRANCE GARDEN
FOR BETH

So the spring days came and went, the sky grew clearer, the earth greener, the flowers were up fair and early and the birds came back in time to say good-by to Beth . . .
—Little Women, Chapter Forty

Never recovering fully from her serious case of scarlet fever three years before, Beth died in the dawn of a spring morning, in the arms of her mother. The snowdrops that "blossomed freshly at the window" would forever be associated with that moment.

Beth loved flowers and, even when she was too weak to go outside to enjoy them, would look down on the garden from her window during the day and at night when she couldn't sleep.

As a reminder of Beth's pure, gentle spirit, plant a little garden of all-white spring flowers such as white bleeding-heart, hyacinths, tulips, narcissi, crocus, lilies of the valley, grape hyacinths, and, of course, snowdrops. The flowers will bloom early in the spring in memory of Beth, the daughter her father called "Little Tranquility" for her "shy manner, timid voice, and peaceful expression, which was seldom disturbed."

In the fall, dig a small bed for planting bulbs. White bleeding-heart will be about eighteen inches high, so plant it in the center of the bed or at the back. Next, plant the white hyacinths, tulips, and narcissi and, finally, toward the front or around the border, plant the smallest bulbs—crocus, lilies of the valley, white grape hyacinths, and snowdrops. Plant the bulbs about four to six inches deep (plant the larger bulbs deeper than the small ones), flat side down. Cover them with soil. Water them well and spread a blanket of leaves or straw over the bed to keep the bulbs snug for winter.

When the tips of the leaves begin to show in early spring, carefully remove the leaves or straw and soon the flowers will bloom.

After the flowers have finished blooming, snip off the stems but let the green leaves of the plants die down naturally so that you will have flowers again the next spring.

If you wish to keep the memory garden blooming over the summer, plant dainty white "annuals" in the same bed—impatiens, pansies, alyssum, and even the silvery white leaves of dusty miller would be ideal choices and would be especially fitting for remembering gentle Beth.

This romantic white garden will be pretty even at night, for it will softly reflect the glow of the moonlight. You will enjoy looking at it from *your* window before you go to sleep.

CONCLUSION

The world of *Little Women*, *Little Men*, and *Jo's Boys* is one of discovery. For the March girls, there were the discoveries of themselves. They learned through reflection and experience what their own talents, as well as their limitations, were. Then they learned how best to make use of their talents and how to overcome their limitations.

For the reader, there is even more to discover. Not only do we learn from the characters in the stories about self-discovery; we also learn about a time and place in history that shaped a whole nation's character. Through the story of Meg, Jo, Beth, and Amy, we can see life as it was in another era and, perhaps more importantly, how life today can be enriched by bringing some of that world into our own.